An Assessment of U.S. Hazardous Materials Emergency Response Preparedness, 1994

Research • Analysis • Synthesis • Planning • Training

Stephan A. Parker

DEDICATION

To my wife Deborah Jean Choupin, who makes all seem possible,

and

my father Frank Leon Parker for setting such a spectacular example

ABSTRACT

ABSTRACT

AN ASSESSMENT OF U.S. HAZARDOUS MATERIALS

EMERGENCY RESPONSE PREPAREDNESS

STEPHAN ALEXANDER PARKER

Thesis under the direction of Professor Mark Abkowitz

Hazardous materials emergency response preparedness is perceived by the public as inadequate, attributed in part to the lack of consolidated information. The objective of this thesis is to investigate this position by conducting an assessment of U.S. hazardous materials emergency response preparedness. The study focused on the role of public emergency response in hazardous materials risk management in the United States, the preparedness of emergency responders to minimize the effects of hazardous materials incidents, and the effectiveness of hazardous materials emergency response in the context of risk management based on empirical analysis.

A 1993-1994 survey database is analyzed to identify current public hazardous materials emergency response competencies. Emergency Response Notification System data from 1986 to 1994 are used to characterize response needs.

It is concluded that Federal initiatives have succeeded in consolidating statistical reporting, and appear to have effectively: (1) addressed the accident and release prevention segments of hazardous materials risk management, and (2) reduced the consequences of hazardous materials releases through improved hazardous materials emergency response (implied by the significant reduction in notification times and increased response team competencies).

i

PAGE LEFT INTENTIONALLY BLANK

ACKNOWLEDGMENTS

Dr. William Bowlby of the Vanderbilt Engineering Center for Transportation Operations and Research (VECTOR) and its Vanderbilt Information Systems in Transportation Academy (VISTA) program made it possible for me to return to school after nine years. Dr. Mark Abkowitz provided invaluable advice and sharpened my focus on the analytical portion, and allowed a non-engineer the latitude to develop the broader perspective crucial to assessing technological systems from a management perspective. I am grateful to Dr. Bob Stammer for his constant reminding that the world moves forward on the basis of decisions, not plans. Elgan Usrey and the Tennessee Emergency Management Agency (TEMA) provided support to VECTOR, which supported me in my work.

Dr. Bruce Cooil of the Owen Graduate School of Management (OGSM) encouraged a healthy skepticism in the validity of statistics, together with the tools to analyze them. OGSM Adjunct Professor Foster instilled an appreciation of the power of the law to inform business actions.

I am indebted to Mark Lepofsky and Kathleen Hancock, whose friendships allowed for free-wheeling discussion of the applicability of their research to the "real-world" decision-making environment.

Most of all I am grateful for the love and support of my family. My wife allowed me to tear her away from her Jackson Hole home of 16 years to pursue my interest in becoming a credentialed transportation professional, and together with my parents supported and encouraged my education.

TABLE OF CONTENTS

LIST OF FIGURES

LIST OF ABBREVIATIONS

AAI...Abkowitz and Associates, Inc.

CERCLA.........Comprehensive Environmental Response, Compensation and Liability Act

CHEMNET..Chemical Industry Mutual Aid Network

CHEMTREC..Chemical Transportation Emergency Center

CPG..Community Planning Guide

DOT..Department of Transportation

EPA..Environmental Protection Agency

EPCRA....................................Emergency Planning and Community Right-to-Know Act

ERNS...Emergency Response Notification System

FEMA..Federal Emergency Management Agency

FY..Federal Fiscal Year

GAO...General Accounting Office

HMTUSA...........................Hazardous Materials Transportation and Uniform Safety Act

ICS...Incident Command System

LEPC..Local Emergency Planning Committee

MSDS...Material Safety Data Sheet

NCP...National Contingency Plan

NFPA...National Fire Protection Association

NRC..National Response Center

NRT...National Response Team

OPA..Oil Pollution Act

OSC...Federal On-Scene Commander

OTA...Office of Technology Assessment

RCRA..Resource Conservation and Recovery Act

RRT..Regional Response Team

SARA...Superfund Amendments and Reauthorization Act

SERC..State Emergency Response Commission

TITLE III..See EPCRA

TRB...Transportation Research Board

TRR...Transportation Research Record

CHAPTER I

EMERGENCY RESPONSE IN THE CONTEXT OF U.S. HAZARDOUS

MATERIALS RISK MANAGEMENT

Fear and Legislation Lead to Planning

Since the Bhopal, India tragedy killed over 2,000 people in 1984, managing hazardous materials risks in the United States has become a high priority for businesses, regulators, and emergency response personnel. Liability for hazardous materials incidents[1] has gained the attention of hazardous materials producers (see Figure 1) and transporters. Similarly, legislative initiatives have focused on emergency preparedness. Notable among these is the Superfund Amendments and Reauthorization Act of 1986 (SARA), which included as Title III the Emergency Planning and Community Right-to-Know Act (EPCRA). EPCRA focused on fixed facility emergency response planning at the local level, with an emphasis on coordinating community resources. EPCRA also required facilities to report the presence and quantities of hazardous materials and releases in order to facilitate emergency response planning, and required the facility to prepare an emergency response plan (see Figure 2). The Oil Pollution Act of 1990 (OPA) effectively extended Federal reporting requirements to include petroleum and non-petroleum oil products.

The threat of a hazardous materials calamity was perceived in the mid-1980s to be greatest while in transportation (see Figure 3). The Hazardous Materials Transportation and Uniform Safety Act of 1990 (HMTUSA) addressed these fears. HMTUSA was the first major amendment of the Hazardous Materials Transportation Act since first passed in 1974. The deregulation of trucking in 1980 was among the destabilizing factors

---

[1] A hazardous materials incident is defined by the National Fire Protection Association as "an emergency involving the release or potential release of a hazardous material, with or without fire"(NFPA *Hazardous Materials Response Handbook*, 1993, p. 17).

SOURCES: Environmental Protection Agency, SPN Directory of Chemical Producers, Chemical Week Buyers Guide, Chemsources U.S.A., individual chemical companies.

Figure 1. Hazardous materials distributors and processors are clustered in distinct geographic groupings, with notable concentrations in Corpus Christi-New Orleans, New York-New Jersey, and Los Angeles. Source: U.S. Congress, Office of Technology Assessment, *Transportation of Hazardous Materials*, OTA-SET-304 (Washington, DC: U.S. Government Printing Office, July 1986), p. 15.

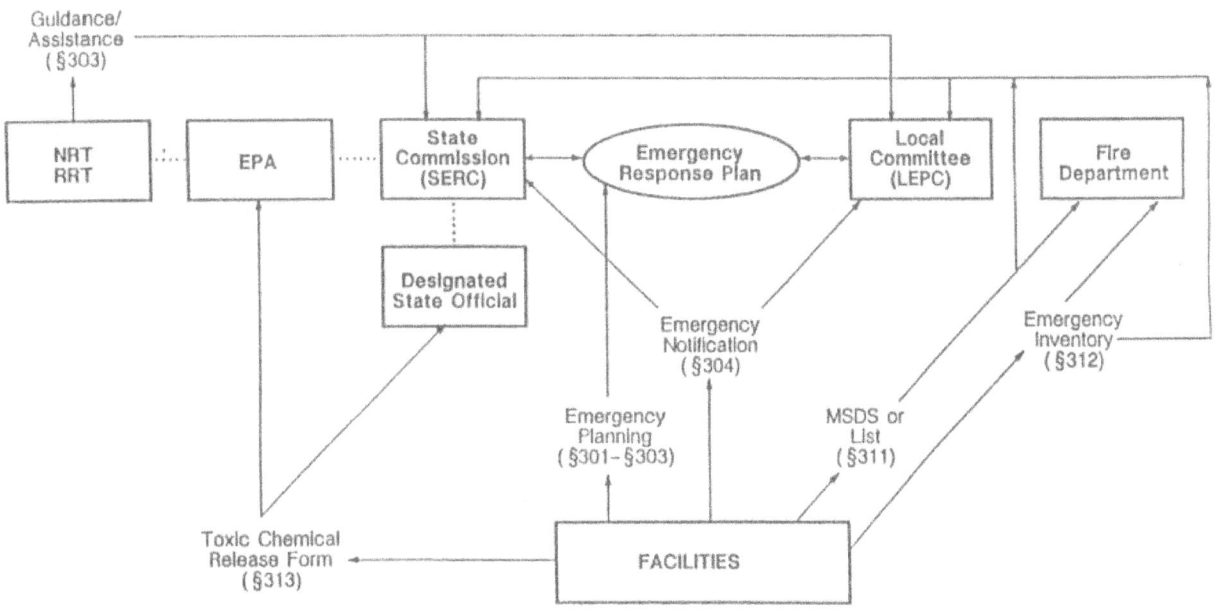

Figure 2. Major information flow requirements of the Emergency Planning and Community Right-to-Know Act of 1986 (EPCRA, or SARA Title III) are displayed graphically here. Source: National Response Team, *Hazardous Materials Emergency Planning Guide* (NRT-1, March 1987), p. A-11.

Hazard	Number of Jurisdictions
1. Nuclear attack......................	a
2. Hazardous materials—highway incident	2,791
3. Winter storm	2,569
4. Flood	2,206
5. Hazardous materials—rail incident	2,188
6. Tornado	2,162
7. Hazardous materials—stationary incident	2,026
8. Urban fire.........................	1,877
9. Wildfire...........................	1,519
10. Hazardous materials—pipeline incident	1,509

[a] All jurisdictions are subject to the effects of nuclear attack.

SOURCE: Jurisdiction responses to Federal Emergency Management Agency, Hazardous Incident Capability Assessment Multi-Year Development Plan, 1985.

Figure 3. The Ten Hazards Perceived as Most Significant by Local Jurisdictions. FEMA's focus on nuclear threats apparently led them to supply perceived hazard number one. Source: U.S. Congress, Office of Technology Assessment, *Transportation of Hazardous Materials*, OTA-SET-304 (Washington, DC: U.S. Government Printing Office, July 1986), p. 218.

contributing to the perception of unsafe transportation. The Federal government has responded with (among other initiatives) accident prevention through more qualified drivers with uniform minimum Commercial Drivers Licenses requirements (effective April, 1992), and hazardous materials release prevention with performance-oriented packaging requirements (rules promulgated in 1990, effective 1996) (see Figure 4).

Whether an incident takes place at a fixed facility or while in transport, though, the individuals most likely to be exposed are employees and emergency response personnel. Minimizing the consequences of hazardous materials incidents through optimized emergency response (see Figure 4) is the goal of hazardous materials emergency response preparedness, and is the focus of this thesis. The role of public emergency response in hazardous materials risk management in the United States, the preparedness of emergency responders to minimize the effects of hazardous materials incidents, and the effectiveness of hazardous materials emergency response in the context of risk management based on empirical study are examined in this thesis.

In conducting this effort, a distinction has been made between preparedness and response. Preparedness takes place before there is an emergency, and is comprised of an adequate management capability; coordinated, trained and equipped responders; and access to information. Response is what happens when an actual incident takes place.

Use of Hazardous Materials Creates the Potential for Emergencies

Growing consumer and industrial demand for products that are flammable, poisonous, explosive, corrosive, or otherwise potentially harmful has resulted in greater exposure to manufacture and transport of these commodities.[2]

The American Chemical Society's Chemical Abstract Service lists 10 million chemicals under 15 million names, with as many as 14,000 new chemicals added each

---

[2]DOT/RSPA/OHMT-89-02 Guidelines for Applying Criteria to Designate Routes for Transporting Hazardous Materials, July 1989, p.2.

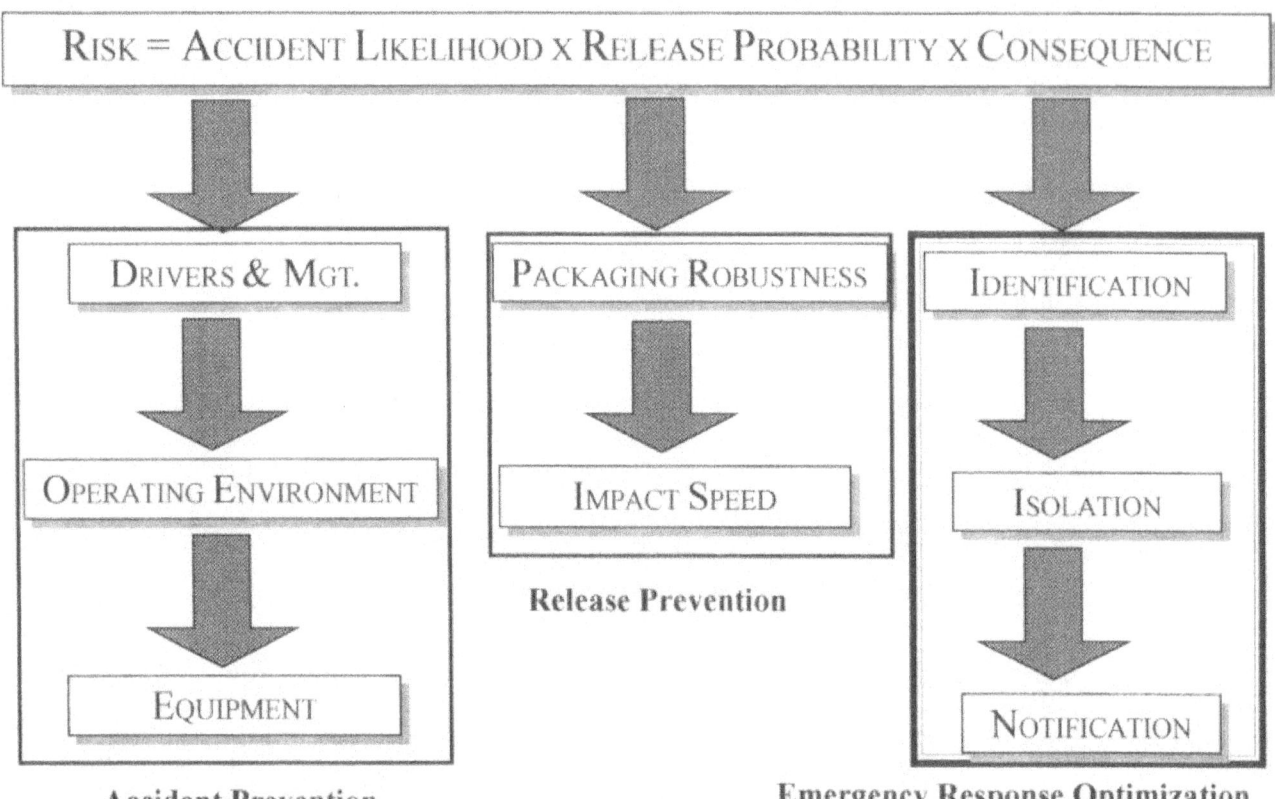

Figure 4. This schematic of an expected risk equation is useful for characterizing risk management activities. This thesis focuses on minimizing consequences through emergency response optimization.

week.[3] As of July 1990, over 100,000 chemicals were regarded as hazardous, with 366 considered extremely hazardous.[4] There are currently 783 substances designated as CERCLA hazardous substances under 40 CFR Part 302.[5] In the transport sector alone, the Department of Transportation (DOT) estimates that over 500,000 movements of hazardous materials occur each day in the United States, with over 4 billion tons moving each year.[6]

The need for specific planning for hazardous materials emergency response was recognized and required in SARA Title III. Congress required the National Response Team (a 14-agency policy board chaired by the Environmental Protection Agency) to publish guidelines that Local Emergency Planning Committees (LEPCs) could use to make effective preparations. The EPA and the U.S. Coast Guard share responsibility for chairing each of the Regional Response Teams (RRTs) that function in an advisory role to State Emergency Response Commissions (SERCs) also created under EPCRA. SERCs, in turn, are to designate Local Emergency Planning Committees (LEPCs), which are responsible for planning emergency response both for specific facilities and for the community as a whole. Guidelines for planning community emergency response are contained in *FEMA's Guide for Development of State and Local Emergency Operations Plans* (CPG 1-8). The *Hazardous Materials Emergency Planning Guide* (NRT-1) issued in March 1987 gave guidance for local emergency plan development (see Figure 5), and was followed in May 1988 by *Criteria for Review of Hazardous Materials Emergency Plans* (NRT-1A). NRT-1A was written primarily for use by RRTs in evaluating state-wide plans, and secondarily for SERCs to use in evaluating LEPC plans.

---

[3]Statement of George Miller on behalf of the National Association of State Fire Marshalls before the Subcommittee on Surface Transportation, Hazardous Materials Transportation, Senate Hearing 101-955, July 25, 1990, p. 247.

[4]Ibid.

[5]EPA, CERCLA Notifications: Emergency Response Notification System (ERNS) Fact Sheet (Publication 9360.0-23FS), April 1992.

[6]Hazardous Materials Transportation Act Amendments of 1993, House Report 103-336 Pt.1, p.3.

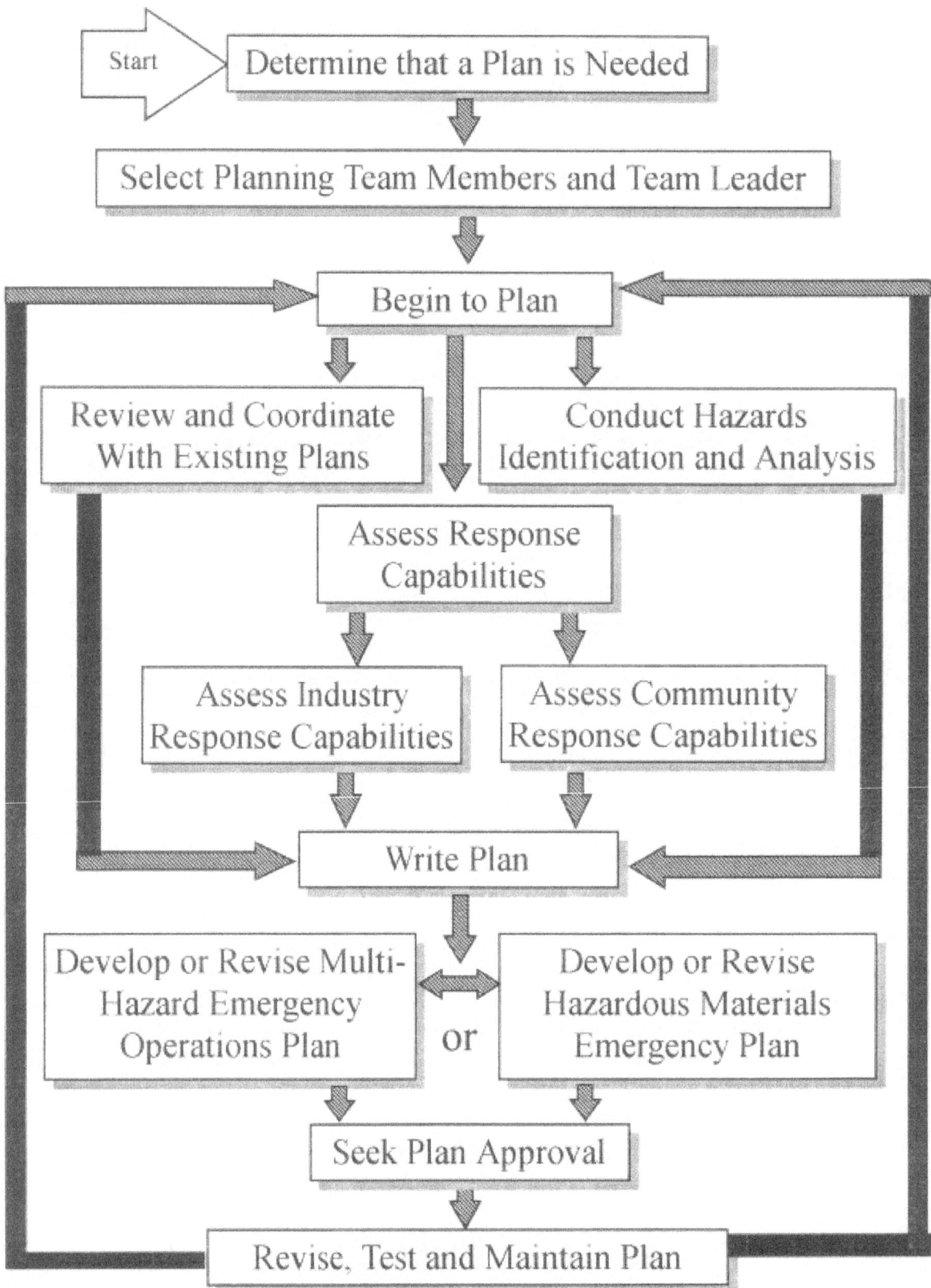

Figure 5. This overview of the emergency response planning process makes it clear that the crucial first step is to determine that a plan is needed. Source: National Response Team, *Hazardous Materials Emergency Planning Guide* (NRT-1, March 1987), p. 3.

LEPCs are required to form a planning team, perform an annual review of the local emergency response plan, and carry out training exercises. Such exercises are intended to test the effectiveness of the local emergency response plan. LEPCs are expected to draw on the information provided in reporting requirements of EPCRA, but may also turn to national resources, such as the Chemical Transportation Emergency Center (CHEMTREC), which operates a non-emergency information hotline that will provide (among other items) Material Safety Data Sheets (MSDS)[7] on any of the more than one million on file.

NRT-1A has a checklist format that shows what is needed in a local hazardous materials emergency response plan, and documents the source of the requirement for specific provisions. It incorporates the general provisions of EPCRA (as Title III), NRT-1, and CPG 1-8. Simply adhering to the checklist, though, is not enough to assure community preparedness. As the National Response Team states, "One of the major themes of NRT-1 is that the way in which a local hazardous materials emergency plan is developed is as important as the actual contents of such a plan."[8]

An explicit step in developing a local emergency plan is assessing both industry (Figure 6) and public (Figure 7) response capabilities.

Effective Emergency Response Minimizes Consequences

The foundation of effective emergency response is to minimize consequences in three steps: (1) identify the hazard sufficiently to determine the appropriate initial response actions, (2) isolate the hazard from people and the environment, and (3) notify authorities to bring in qualified ultimate responders (see Figure 8). Compressing the time for each step, and therefore the overall process, limits the consequences (see Figure 9). Delays at

---

[7]"Material Safety Data Sheet (MSDS). A form, provided by manufacturers and compounders (blenders) of chemicals, with minimum information about chemical composition, physical and chemical properties, health and safety hazards, emergency response, and waste disposal of the material as required by OSHA 1910.1200." NFPA *Hazardous Materials Response Handbook*, 1993, p. 125.
[8]NRT-1A, p.4.

▲ CHEMNET chemical industry emergency response teams
■ CHEMNET contractor emergency response teams

SOURCE: Chemical Manufacturers Association.

Figure 6. CHEMNET emergency response teams in 1985 tended to cluster near fixed facilities. Source: U.S. Congress, Office of Technology Assessment, *Transportation of Hazardous Materials*, OTA-SET-304 (Washington, DC: U.S. Government Printing Office, July 1986), p. 17.

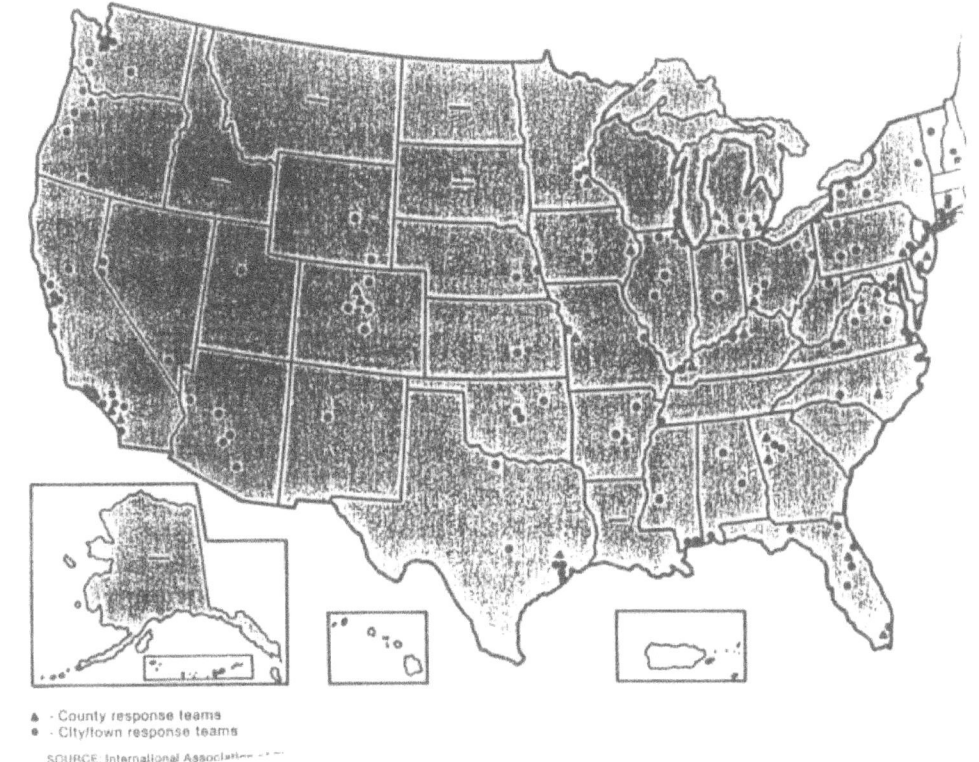

Figure 7. There were only about 130 public hazardous materials response teams identified in 1985. Source: U.S. Congress, Office of Technology Assessment, *Transportation of Hazardous Materials*, OTA-SET-304 (Washington, DC: U.S. Government Printing Office, July 1986), p. 16.

FOUNDATION ELEMENTS OF HAZARDOUS MATERIALS EMERGENCY RESPONSE

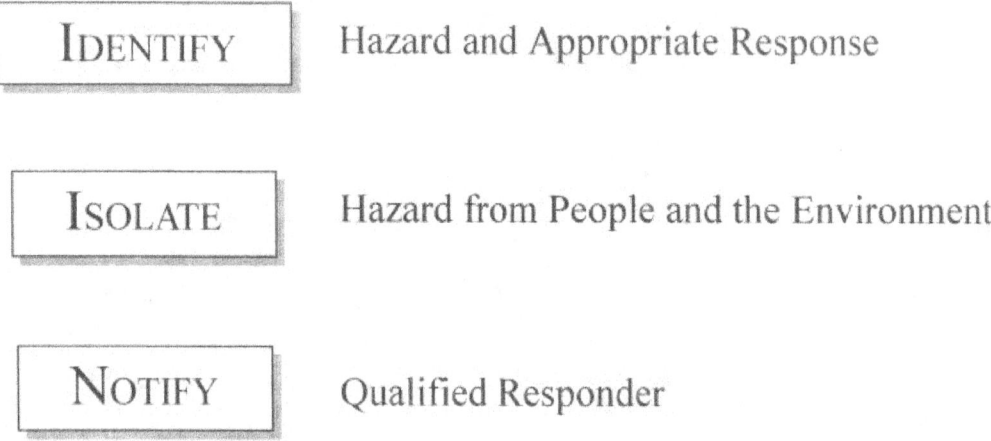

IDENTIFY — Hazard and Appropriate Response

ISOLATE — Hazard from People and the Environment

NOTIFY — Qualified Responder

Figure 8. These three foundation elements are at the heart of effective first response. Compressing these steps over time generally minimizes consequences.

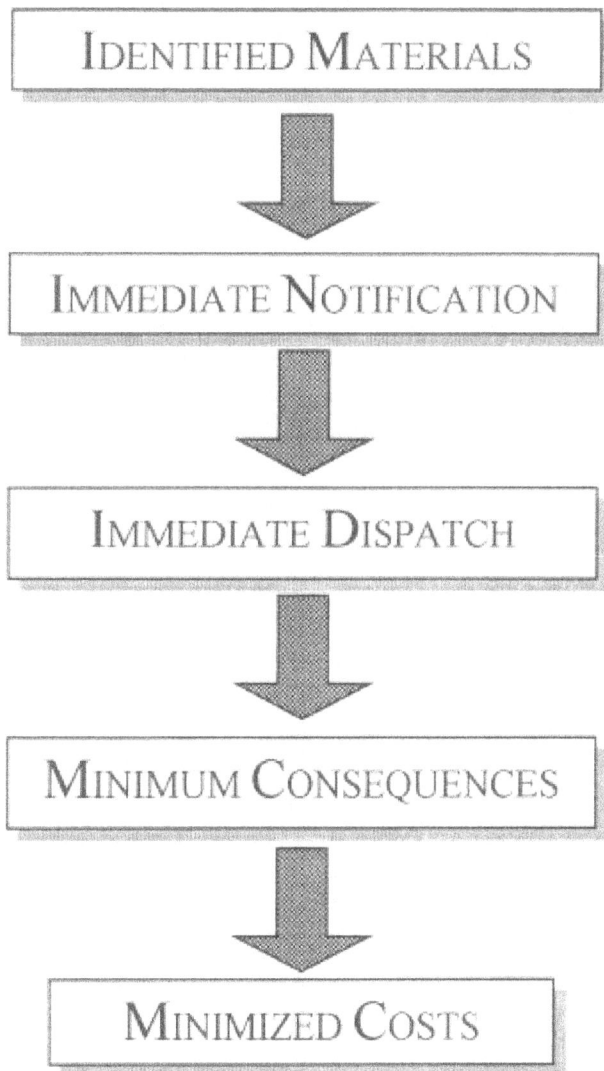

Figure 9. Incident consequences are minimized when notification and response time are compressed.

any stage propagate, increasing the consequence severity (see Figure 10). Thus, there is significant motivation to plan for time-efficient emergency response.

Producers of hazardous materials are required to have emergency response plans available for emergency responders filed with LEPCs. Each of these plans may be unique, as it is facility-specific, and may be chemical-specific within the facility. According to the level of expertise deemed necessary for adequate response, the plan may call for various company personnel to join local emergency response crews, industrial mutual aid response, or regional response. For some hazards, the Federal government reserves the right to send its own On-Scene Commander (OSC) to oversee cleanup. Federal OSCs may come from the Environmental Protection Agency (EPA), Coast Guard, Department of Energy or Department of Defense, depending on the material and quantity involved. Decisions to send an OSC are made in most cases at the EPA regional offices after being notified by the National Response Center. The National Response Center may also activate the NRT or RRT to provide technical assistance. All of these more-involved responses are likely to take hours or days to occur.

Size of the Emergency Response Community

The primary components of emergency response are found on the first page of your phone book: fire service, police, medical service. Any of these services may receive the initial call to a hazardous materials incident, and they are treated as a group as "first responders." The objective of hazardous materials emergency response is to protect people, property and the environment by minimizing the exposure to hazardous materials. Training all of the two million first responders to look for signs and to recognize the presence of hazardous materials is the first step. The National Fire Protection Association calls this the "Awareness" level of training, and recommends training to this level for anyone likely to be first on the scene of a hazardous materials spill, leak, fire or exposure, including truck drivers and train crews.

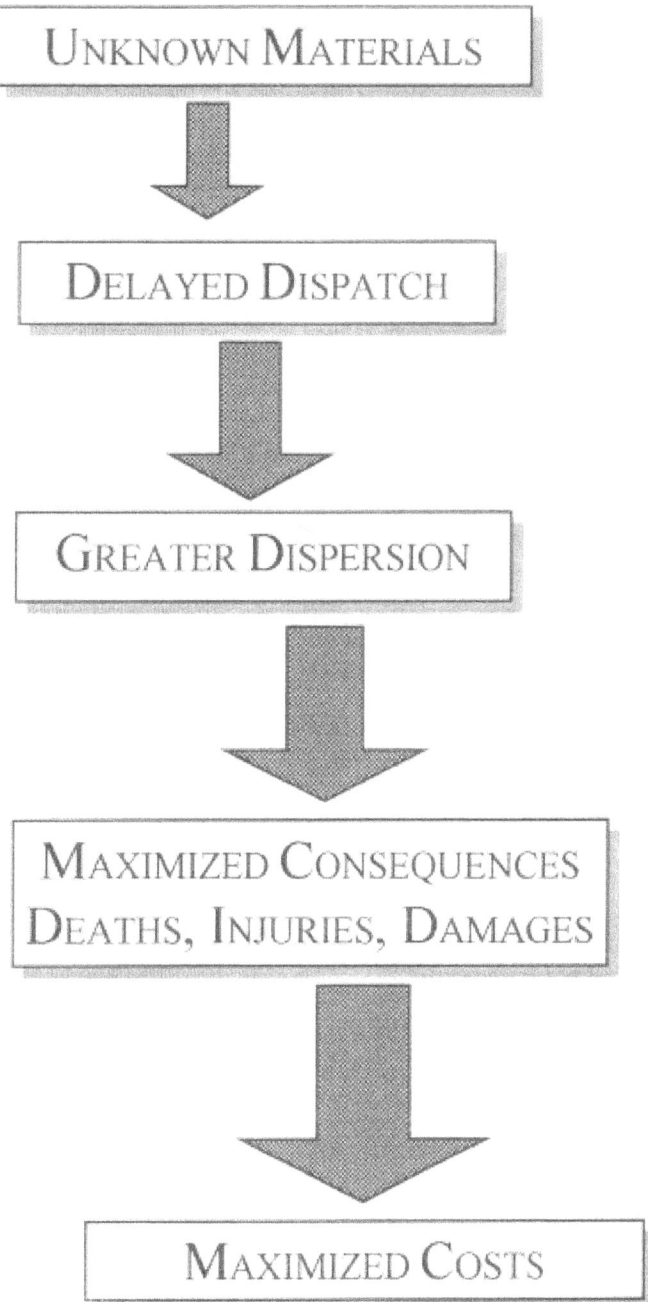

Figure 10. Incident consequences tend to expand when notification and response time are not compressed.

Some 450,000 to 500,000 local law enforcement officers and approximately 400,000 basic emergency medical technicians are likely to be first responders.[9] The International Association of Fire Fighters represents 180,000 professional fire fighters in the U.S.[10] The National Volunteer Fire Council represents more than 1 million volunteer fire fighters in the U.S.[11] The National Association of State Fire Marshalls estimates there are approximately 30,000 fire departments in the U.S.[12] Fire department personnel are primarily concerned with public safety from buildings on fire, and training focuses on "structural fire fighting." Providing this most basic service is so expensive that about 85 percent of the fire fighters in the U.S. are volunteers.[13] The Office of Technology Assessment estimated in 1986 that *at most* only 25 percent of the 2 million first responders (see Figure 11) had adequate training.[14]

---

[9]U.S. Congress, Office of Technology Assessment, *Transportation of Hazardous Materials*, OTA-SET-304 (Washington, DC: U.S. Government Printing Office, July 1986), p. 203.
[10]Subcommittee on Surface Transportation, Hazardous Materials Transportation, Senate Hearing 101-955, July 25, 1990, p.230.
[11]Subcommittee on Surface Transportation, Hazardous Materials Transportation, Senate Hearing 101-955, July 25, 1990, p.241.
[12]Subcommittee on Surface Transportation, Hazardous Materials Transportation, Senate Hearing 101-955, July 25, 1990, p.247.
[13]U.S. Congress, Office of Technology Assessment, *Transportation of Hazardous Materials*, OTA-SET-304 (Washington, DC: U.S. Government Printing Office, July 1986), p. 203.
[14]U.S. Congress, Office of Technology Assessment, *Transportation of Hazardous Materials*, OTA-SET-304 (Washington, DC: U.S. Government Printing Office, July 1986), p. 9.

The First Responder Community

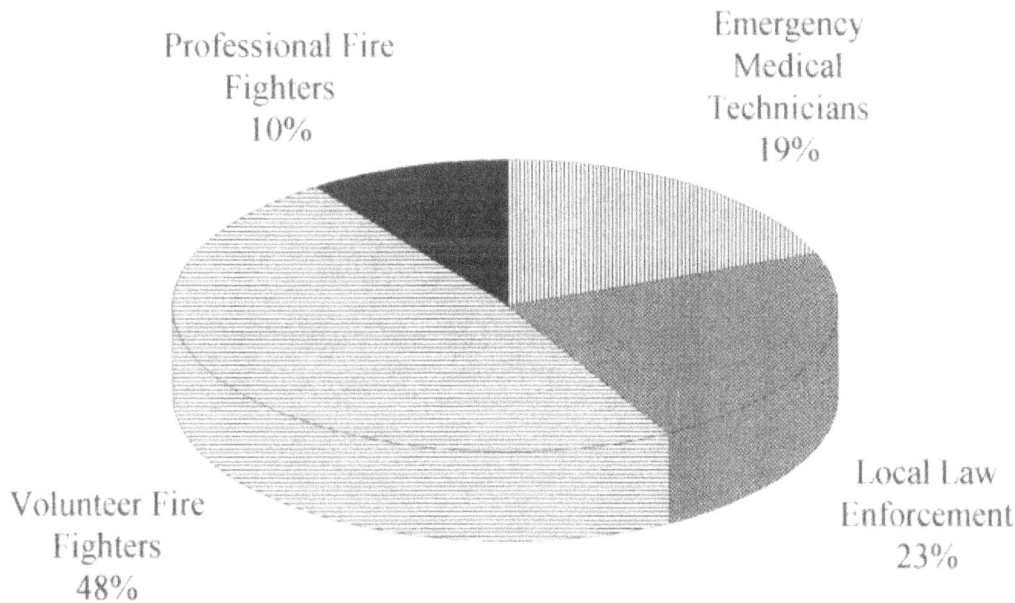

Figure 11. The first responder community consists of about one million volunteer fire fighters, 450,000 to 500,000 local law enforcement officers, 400,000 emergency medical technicians, and 200,000 professional fire fighters

CHAPTER II

ASSESSING U.S. HAZARDOUS MATERIALS EMERGENCY

RESPONSE PREPAREDNESS

Study Methodology

The aforementioned review of the emergency response community is not a census of what exists in the United States today. A 1985 study by the International Association of Fire Chiefs identified approximately 130 public hazardous materials response teams,[15] shown in Figure 7. To update the inventory for 1994, a study funded by Abkowitz and Associates, Inc.(AAI) attempted to identify the location, personnel, training and equipment of every hazardous materials response team in the United States in order to assess their potential response capabilities (see Figure 12).[16] Presented in this section are summary assessments of public hazardous materials response preparedness for the 48 contiguous states and the District of Columbia, based on responses to the AAI survey.

EPCRA required each state's governor to appoint a State Emergency Response Commission (SERC), which in turn was to appoint Local Emergency Planning Committees (LEPCs) to cover all areas of the state. These LEPCs are charged with planning and coordinating local emergency response plans under planning guidelines issued by the National Response Team.

It seemed logical that the way to find all hazardous materials response teams in the U.S. would be through the National Response Team, but they do not keep a registry. Neither do the various fire industry trade associations. The National Response Team did provide a contact list of all SERCs, which when contacted were generally able to provide state lists of LEPCs. Most LEPCs contacted could not identify a local hazmat team, and referred inquiries to local fire departments, state police, or state fire marshalls. Where

---

[15]Ibid, p.220.
[16]Unpublished letter from AAI to contacted hazardous materials response teams, 1993.

Steps Involved in Survey Design and Data Collection

Goal: To identify every public hazardous materials response team in the U.S.

♦ Survey Designed to Reflect

1 Institutional Planning and Coordination
2 Specialized Capabilities
3 Communications
4 Training
5 Chemical Protective Clothing
6 Respiratory Equipment
7 Hazard Detectors
8 Containment

♦ Survey Administration

1 Contacted State Emergency Response Commissions for List of LEPCs
2 Asked Local Emergency Planning Committees for Response Agencies
3 Sent Survey to Response Agencies (May 1993 to Present)
4 Wrote and Called Until All Agencies Completed Survey or Declined
5 Data Entry

♦ Data Verification

1 Computer-Generated Filled Form Sent to Interviewee for Verification
2 State List Sent to Interviewees for Peer Check
3 Writing and Calling Until All Agencies Completing Survey Verify
4 Data in Analysis is Pre-verification Data
5 One-third of Verifications Received As of April 12, 1994

Figure 12. The 1993-1994 Abkowitz and Associates, Inc. survey design and data collection effort is still in verification.

LEPCs did identify hazardous materials response teams, questionnaires developed by AAI consultants were sent (see Figure 13). State Police, Highway Patrols, Fire Marshalls, Offices of Emergency Services and other agencies were contacted to try to elicit the identities of all public hazardous materials response teams in each of the 48 contiguous states and the District of Columbia. In many cases, local fire departments had mutual aid agreements with private hazardous materials response teams, in which case such private teams were also contacted and asked to participate in the survey. In the majority of states, telephone interviews with the most informative respondents to information requests helped in the identification of contacts for recognized hazardous materials teams in the state. A copy of the survey form and summary response totals appear in Figure 13.[17]

Data Collection

Once surveys were received and data entered into the database, verification forms (see Appendix A) were sent to the surveyed teams to check for accuracy and completeness; the verification forms had a few new questions and some clarifications based on initial responses. State lists of identified hazardous materials teams were sent to each state's respondents for a peer check to identify missing teams.[18]

1,227 identified entities had responded to the survey as of February 2, 1994. Of these, 793 had at least one person trained in ICS or one of the hazardous materials response designations, or at least one special vehicle, or at least one Level C, B or A protective suit. Having at least one of these qualifications is considered in this analysis as the minimum basis for being considered a hazardous materials emergency response entity with potential hazard mitigation duties. For this reason, keeping the narrower 793 number

---

[17]Bolded numbers indicate affirmative answers; where followed by non-bolded numbers, , enumerative answers have been totaled. Because of the overlapping jurisdictions, these numbers should be viewed cautiously.

[18]Because verification was not completed in time for this thesis, initial responses are used here.

County:	HAZARDOUS MATERIALS	EM USE ONLY
City:	EMERGENCY RESPONSE	Team Level:
Region:	SURVEY	Date:
Date:		Rated By:

Instructions: (1) Please type or print clearly. (2) Complete a separate form for each station/substation with HazMat response capability. (Make additional copies as needed.) (3) Return completed surveys to: Abkowitz & Associates Inc. FAX 800-243-7475 or mail to: Abkowitz & Associates Inc. Attn: Stephan Parker 2100 West End Avenue, Suite 540, Nashville TN 37203.

1. General Information

Department/Agency: 1 _____ Team Leader: 2 _____

Mailing Address: 3 _____ Business Phone: 4 ( ) _____

City: 5 _____ State: 6 _____ Zip: 7 _____ Emergency Phone: 8 ( ) _____

(Other than 911)

FAX Number: 9 ( ) _____

Station Location (Street Address): 10 _____

Location (if known)   Latitude: 11 _____ Longitude: 12 _____

No. Paid: 13 _____ No. Volunteer: 14 _____ No. Assigned to Team: 15 _____ Avg. Response Time: 16 **748** _____

2. Jurisdictional Profile (please include a map indicating boundaries and response stations)

Total Population Served: 17 **832**   152,662,943   Area (square miles): 18 **774**   1,270,212

Major Highways: 19 _____   Major Railroads: 20 _____

Navigable Rivers: 21 _____   Airports: 22 _____

Multi-jurisdictional Response? 23 **611** Yes ____ No   Industrial Mutual Aid Agreement? 24 **274** Yes ____ No

List Jurisdictional(s) served by written mutual aid agreements:

25 _____
_____

Comments:

26 _____
_____
_____
_____

3. Capabilities Assessment

Planning: Has the jurisdiction completed SARA Title III Emergency Management Plan? 27 **756** Yes ____ No

Has the plan been successfully exercised and evaluated? 28 **560** Yes ____ No

Date of last excercise: 29 _____

Medical Surveillance: Are team members participating in a medical surveillance program in accordance with OSHA 1910.120? 30 **610** Yes ____ No

Figure 13. The AAI survey form. **Bolded** numbers are affirmative responses; non-bolded following numbers are cumulative for the responses. Source: Abkowitz and Associates, Inc., 1994.

4. Training: (List the total number of personnel currently trained to the levels listed below. Do not include anyone who has not received initial and/or refresher training in the past two years)

	Awareness		Operations		ICS		Technician		Specialist		Advanced	
Senior Officer: Check if Team Leader 228	224	1,174	284	1,431	398	2,067	312	1,000	177	567	104	258
Team Leader(s)	197	1,247	219	1,753	297	1,764	364	1,858	218	729	71	247
Team Members	263	6,281	331	7,755	282	5,006	518	8,667	206	2,352	87	444
Support Personnel	290	27,405	364	30,207	178	11,676	102	2,271	39	617	16	79
Totals	974	36,107	1198	41,146	1135	20,513	1296	13,796	640	4,265	247	1,028

5. Equipment: (List number of pieces in the appropriate blanks)

PPE	Detectors	Respirators	Containment
Turnouts (SFPC) 713 46,165	Combustable Gas 671 2,591	30 min SCBA 697 21,258	Booms/Pads 546
Level C 434 13,280	Oxygen Level 601 2,033	60 min SCBA 540 7,485	Plugs/Patches 519
Level B 591 12,606	Detector Tubes 460	Air Line 239 8,225	Plastic 457
Level A 552 6,464	Photoionization 162	1/2 Mask Cartridge 105 3,386	Shovels 614
Fire Res Coveralls 395 8,138	Flame Ionization 84	Full Mask Cartrdg 216 4,433	Absorbants 519
Proximity Suit 297 2,060	Organic Vapor 164		Recovery Drums 554
Disposable Suits 555 21,170	CDV-777-1 Kit 406		Solidifiers 175
Cooling Vests 172 963	Rad Hwy Haz Kit 188		Neutralizers 362
Nuke Suits (write-in) 20 139	Strips 241		
	pH Paper 496		

Available Transportation:
No.Equipped Trucks 504 1,557 No.Heavy Equipment 94 2,679 No.Aircraft 35 96 No.Special Vehicles 315 712

Non-Sparking Tools? 101 603 Yes___No   SCBA Refill: Cascade: 111 596 Fixed 112 576 Portable
Decontamination? 102 629 Yes___No   Compressor: 113___Fixed 114___Portable
No. Reference Books? 103 589 11,682   Foam (enter no. of gal): Alcohol: 115 334 Protein: 116 129
  DOT P 5800.5 1990 ERG 104 595 Yes___No   Light water: 117 264 Other: 118___
  List Additional 105___
  106___
  107___
  108___
  109___
  110___

6. Communications/Information Management

Cellular Phone 119 591 Phone Number(s) 120___
Radio: 121 753 Bands(s)/Frequency(s) 122___
FAX: 123 606 Fixed: Phone Number 124___ 125 161 Portable: Phone Number 126___
Computer: 127___Fixed 128 525 IBM compatible 129 171 Apple/Mac
  130___Portable 131 252 IBM compatible 132 117 Apple/Mac
Programs: 133___Cameo 134___Archie 135 573 Plume Modeling 136___EIS 137___Others

7. Survey Completed by:

Print Name___ Title/Rank___ Signature___
Date:___ Phone Number:(___)___

Figure 13, continued.

in mind during descriptions of the national public response capability is an important consideration.

600 Capable Public Response Teams

Figure 14 shows the areas reported, average response times, and completed Emergency Management Plans by jurisdictions per SARA Title III. Only three-fourths (560/756) of those plans had been exercised and evaluated, however. This is probably indicative of the learning curve and the timing of the survey (the verification form, for which responses have not all been received and processed as of this writing, asks for the date of the next scheduled exercise (see Appendix A)). Roughly 600 teams report Medical Surveillance, Multi-Jurisdictional Response, and Decontamination capability (see Figures 14 and 15). These essential functions are definitive of hazardous materials response, suggesting that there are roughly 600 Public Hazardous Materials Response Teams in the United States with competence above and beyond that of the average fire department.

Specialized equipment for decontamination, dedicated trucks, and non-sparking tools (for explosion hazards) are present throughout the competent response community, as seen in Figure 15.

Figure 16 indicates 518 teams have designated team members trained to the Technician level and 206 teams have members trained to the Specialist level. Personnel trained to the indicated levels number close to 14,000 Technicians and over 4,000 Specialists, on top of 41,000 Operations and 36,000 Awareness level trained personnel (see Figure 17).

What does this mean in terms of how many qualified public hazardous materials response teams exist in the U.S. today? There appear to be at least 600 teams competent to effectively respond to hazardous materials incidents, based on survey responses concerning the number of teams with trained personnel, decontamination capability, and

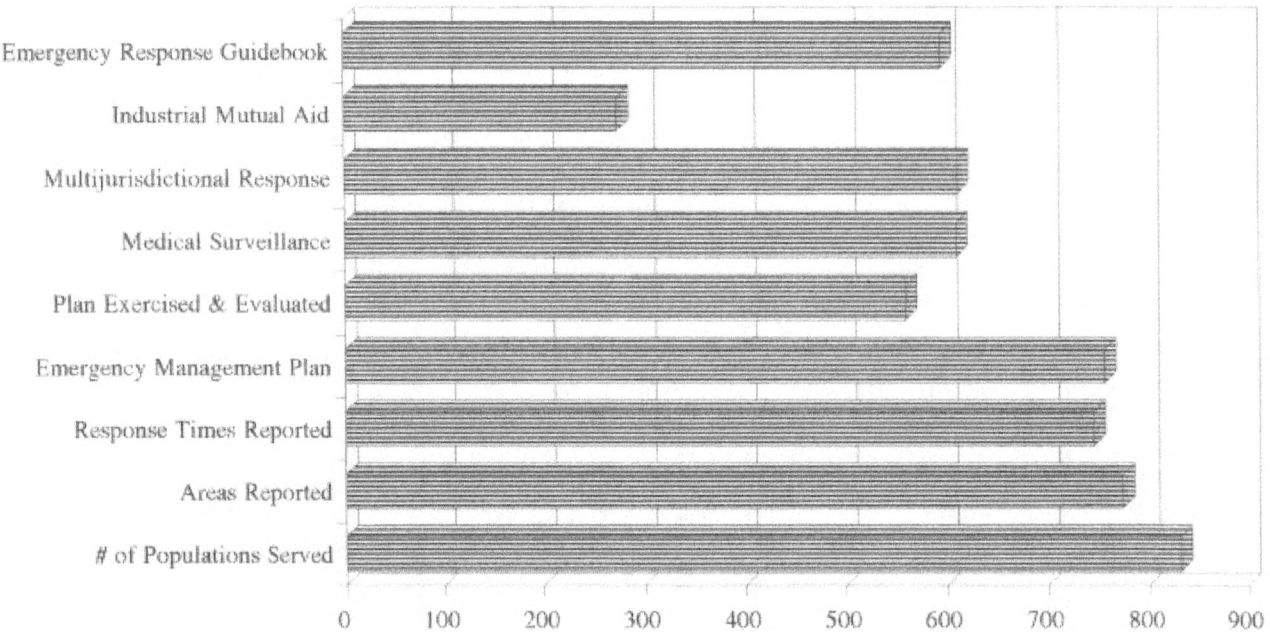

Figure 14. Scope of teams surveyed, 1993-1994. Source: Abkowitz and Associates, Inc, 1994.

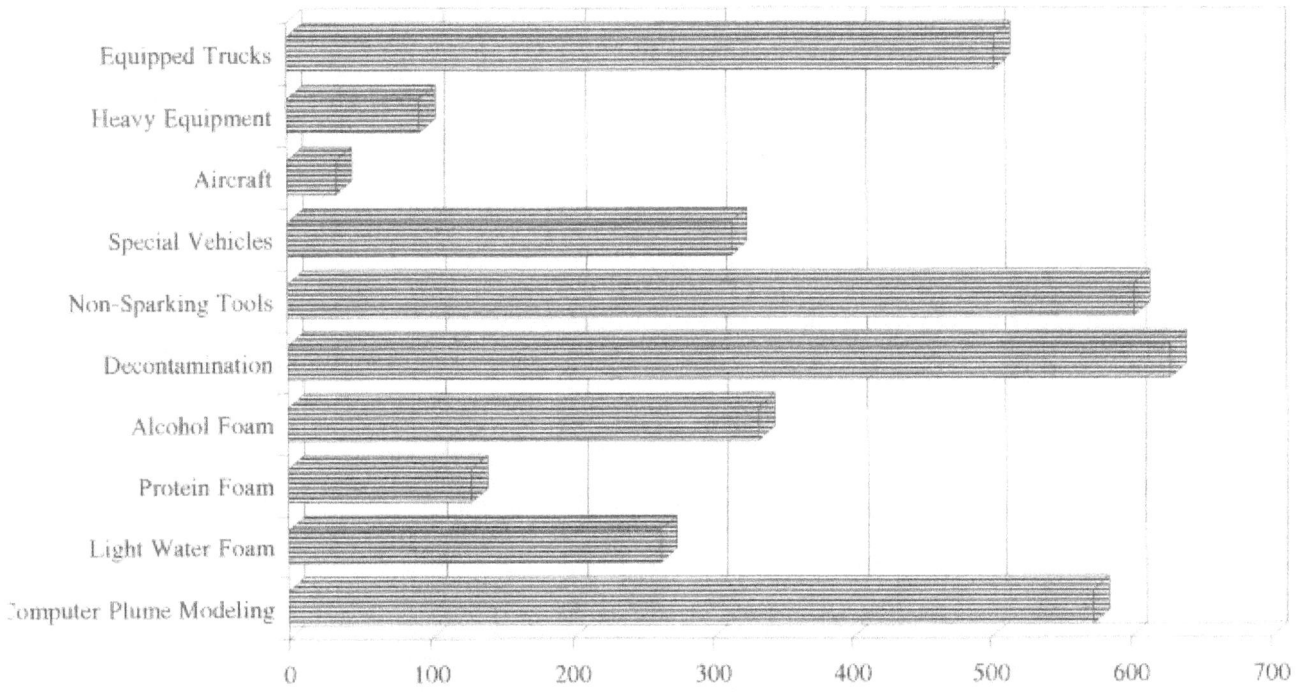

Figure 15. Teams with specialized equipment. Source. Abkowitz and Associates, Inc, 1994

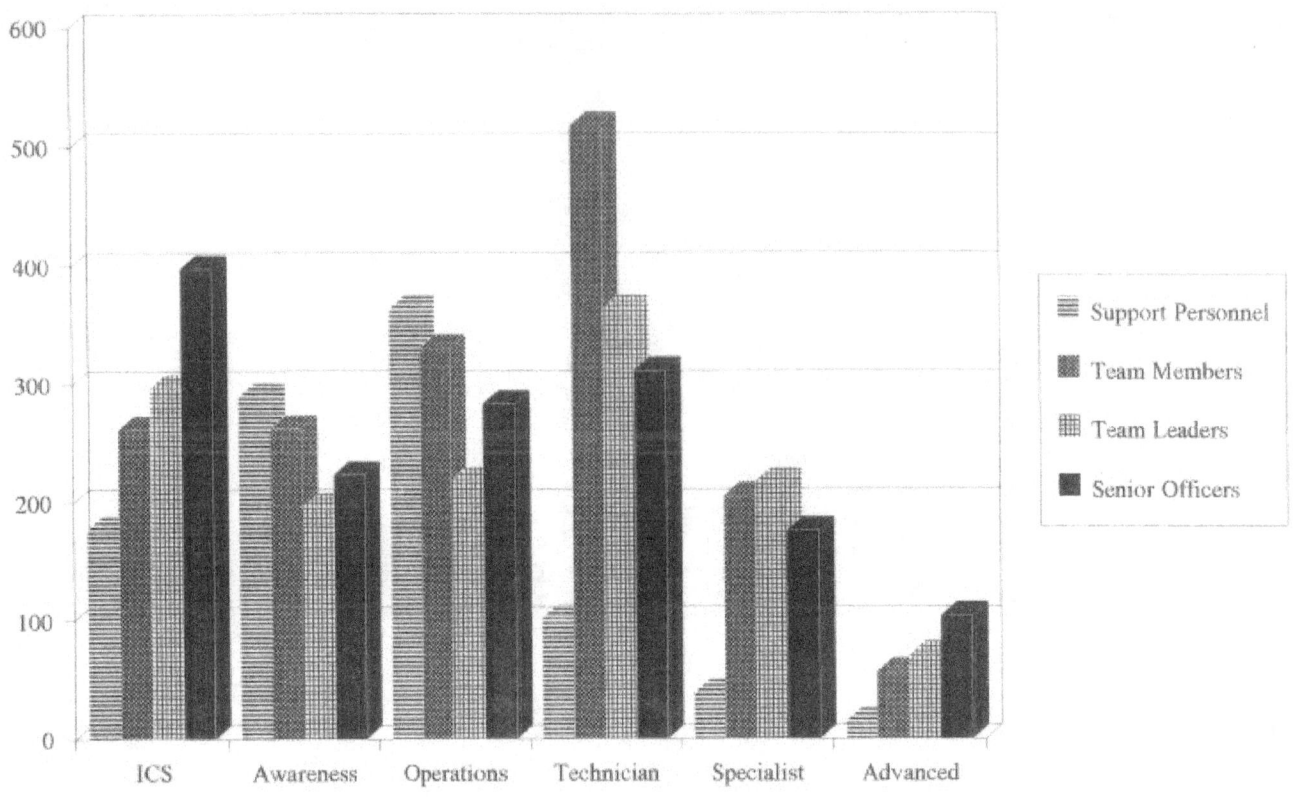

Figure 16. Teams with personnel trained. Source: Abkowitz and Associates, Inc, 1994.

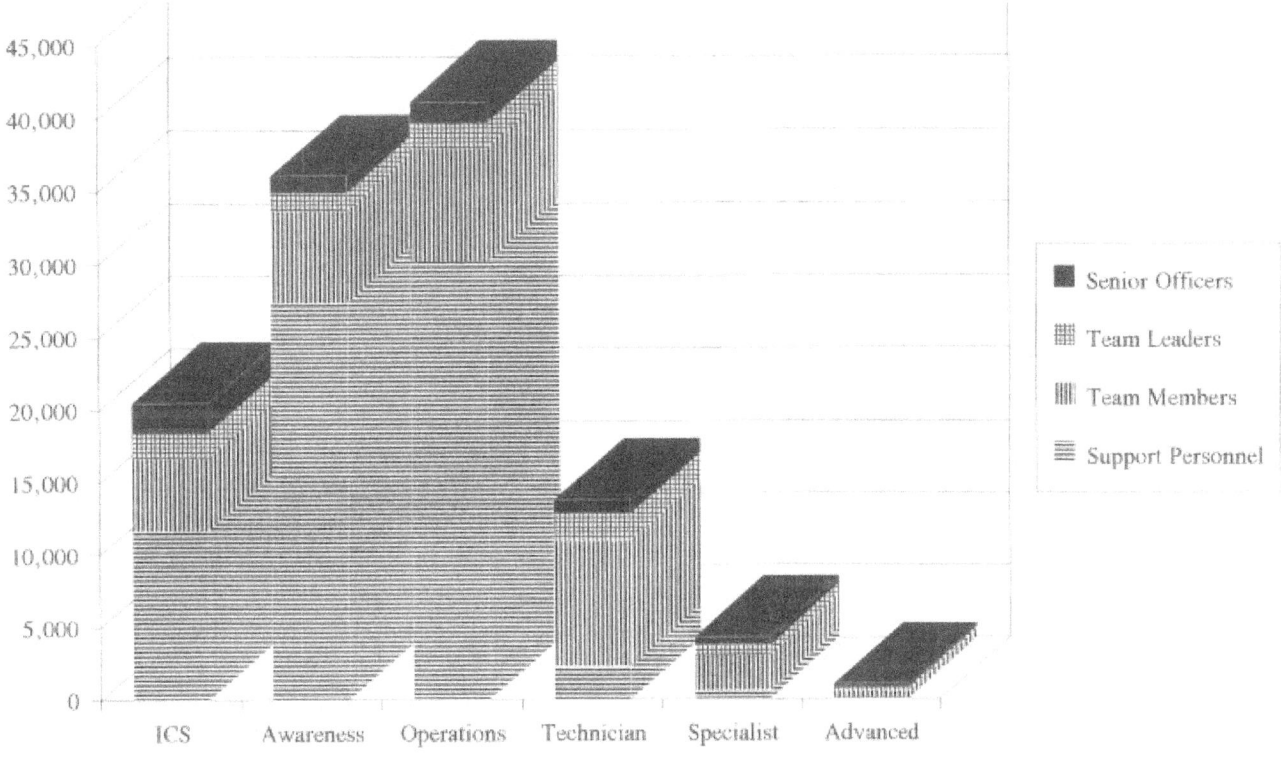

Figure 17. Total personnel trained Source: Abkowitz and Associates, Inc, 1994.

some Level B or A Chemical Protective Clothing and appropriate respiratory gear (see Figures 18-21). Between 150 and 200 of these teams appear to possess significantly greater capabilities, judging from the survey data on specialized chemical detector and containment equipment discussed below. Some 700 organizations surveyed had the Level D (no chemical protection) clothing called "Turnouts," but again 600 showed high-level response capability for chemical hazards: about twice those capable of responding in proximity to high-heat (2,000 degrees Fahrenheit) fires (see Figure 18). Much of the chemical response capability is presumably made through the use of disposable suits. Twenty responders wrote in that they have nuclear response suits.

Figure 20 demonstrates that 30 minute SCBA is ubiquitous, and while there are not 600 response units with 60 minute SCBA, it may not be necessary, given the high degree of SCBA refill capability.

Multi-Jurisdictional, Tiered Response

There is a temptation to assess response in discrete units, but one must keep in mind that response occurs in a continuum. Definitions of "successful" response vary according to the missions of the assessor and responder. First responders are often local fire departments or law enforcement officers, who follow the dictum "safety first," and who are trained to assume the worst case until they have confirmed otherwise. Their primary mission is to protect lives and property. Protecting lives includes protecting responders by not unnecessarily exposing them to hazards.

Key to understanding the national response capability is the recognition that over 600 teams have Multi-Jurisdictional Response Agreements (see Figure 14), which means they share personnel and resources. Thus, individually assessing each responding entity to see if it individually has a Level A protected response capability for Poisonous by Inhalation Gas is to ignore the concept of tiered response.

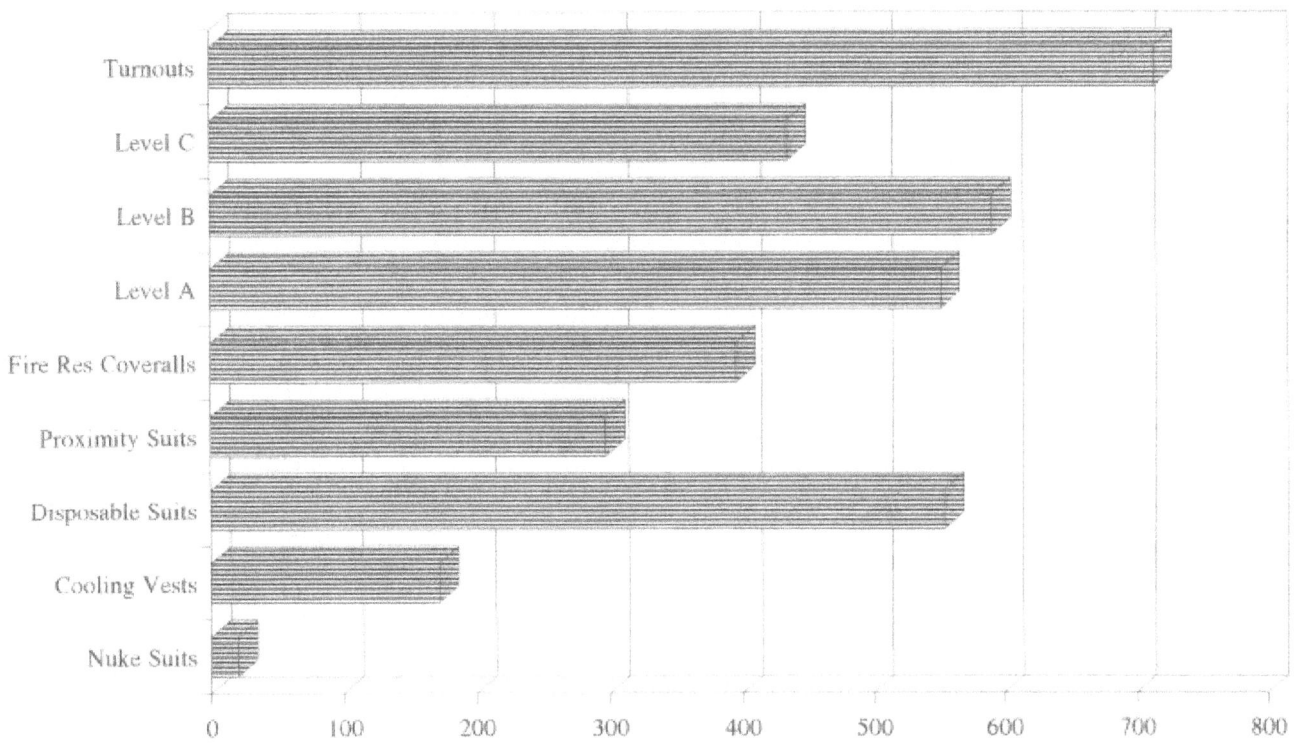

Figure 18. Teams with protective clothing. Source: Abkowitz and Associates, Inc, 1994.

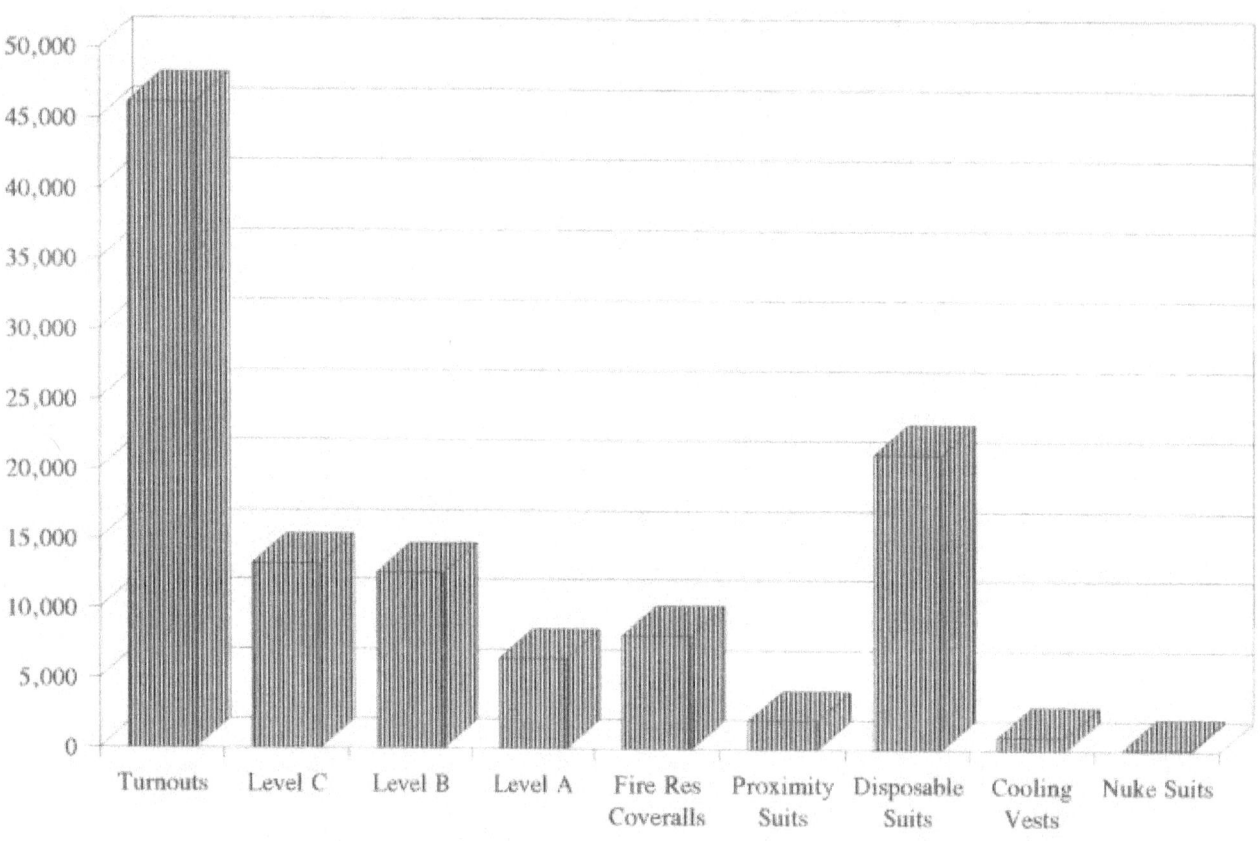

Figure 19. Total protective clothing units. Source: Abkowitz and Associates, Inc, 1994.

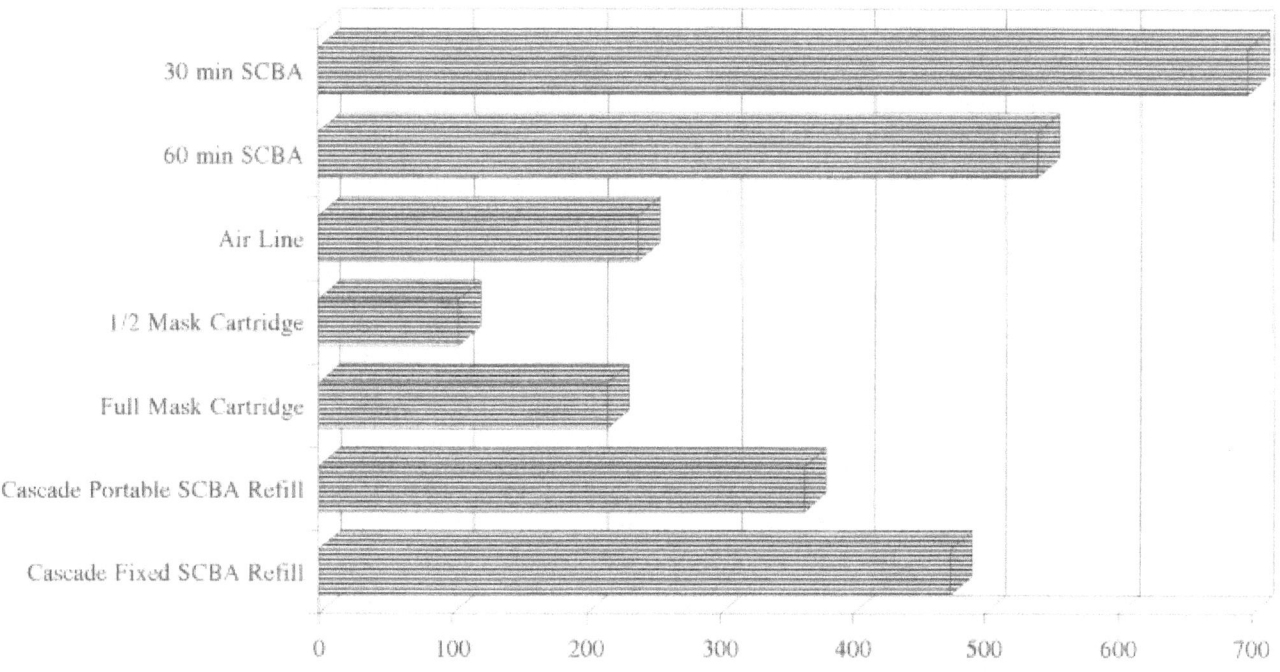

Figure 20. Teams with respirators. Source: Abkowitz and Associates, Inc, 1994.

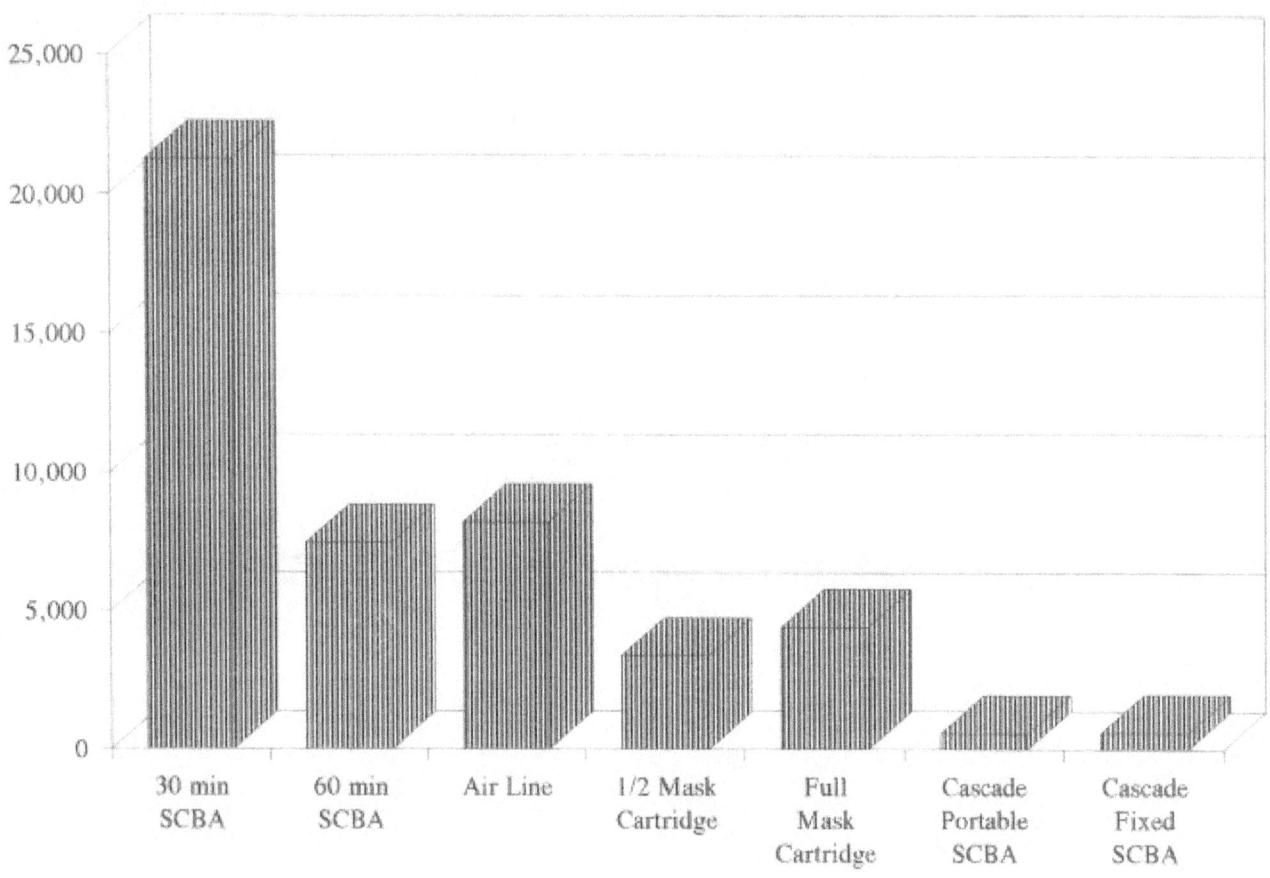

Figure 21. Total respirator units. Source: Abkowitz and Associates, Inc, 1994.

It is also quite likely that the Responsible Party will have plant technicians trained to handle on-site emergencies, who will also respond off-site for their products. The Department of Energy, for example, has over 1,000 facilities with individual chemical hazardous materials response capabilities on-site, and off-site radiological response available.[19]

Besides the CHEMTREC information hotline, the Chemical Manufacturers Association maintains 24-hour dispatch capability for the CHEMNET network of 225 private response teams that will respond upon request of the Responsible Party. This is in addition to the formal industrial mutual aid agreements for such specific products as Chlorine, Phosphorous, Hydrogen Fluoride, Hydrogen Cyanide, Hydrogen Peroxide, and Vinyl Chloride, and similar agreements covering shipments of compressed gases, swimming pool chemicals and liquefied petroleum gas.[20] Over 270 AAI surveyed entities indicated they have Industrial Mutual Aid Agreements, as shown in Figure 14. For all the incidents, accidents and agreements, in 1992 CHEMNET was called to respond to just 7 incidents, and in 1993 to only 4 incidents[21] (see Figure 6 for CHEMNET Team locations), suggesting that local capability is adequate for the vast majority of incidents.

"Preparedness" is defined here as "having the capability to adequately respond to hazardous materials incidents." Adequate local response will vary according to the hazards that are likely to be encountered, and the public response capability will be influenced by the degree of private response preparedness.

Continuing to look at the AAI data, Figure 22 indicates that nearly 600 responders have cellular phones and over 700 have radios, but only about 160 have portable fax machines. This severely limits the immediate usefulness of CHEMTREC-provided

---

[19]Wally Weaver, Director of Emergency Management Division, U.S. Department of Energy. Telephone interview July 14, 1993.
[20]Chemical Manufacturers Association, CHEMTREC (brochure), n.d.
[21]Howard Manning, Manager, CHEMTREC Call Center. Telephone interview March 21, 1994.

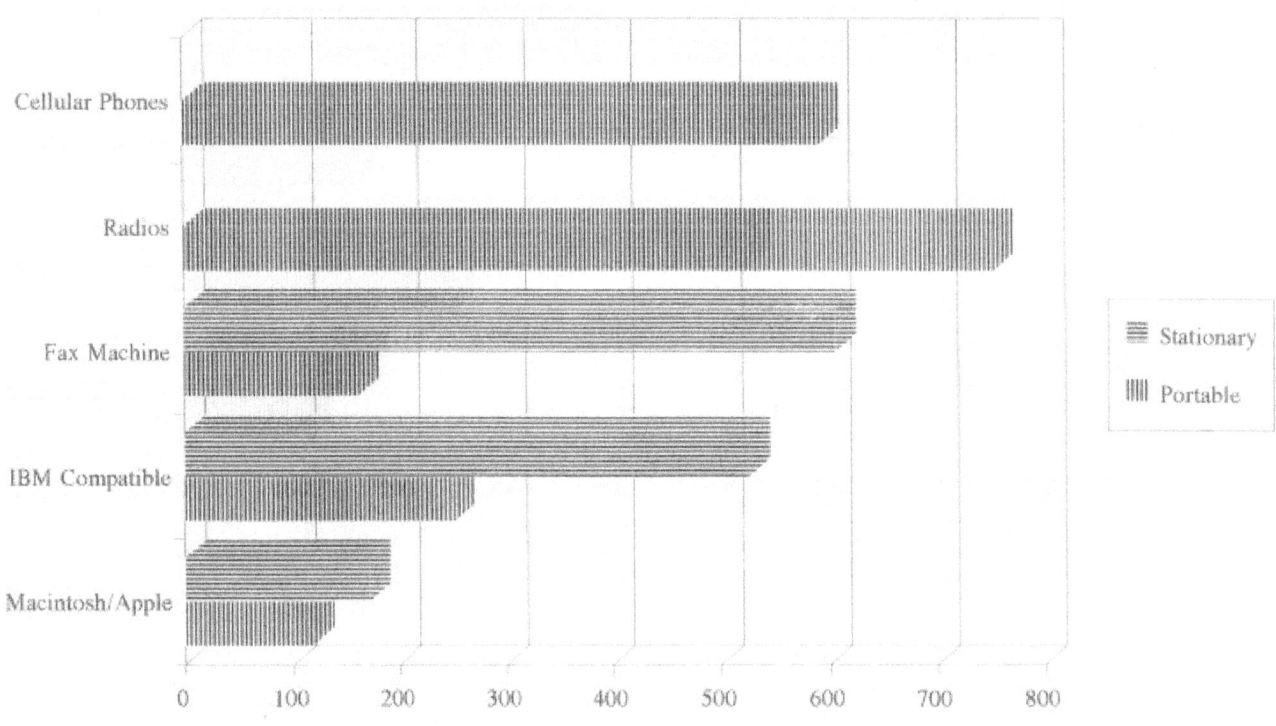

Figure 22. Team communications capabilities. Source: Abkowitz and Associates, Inc, 1994.

Material Safety Data Sheets, for example, because the information would need to be read over the radio or phone, or driven to the scene, once received.

The fire-oriented configuration of the teams is apparent in their detector selection (see Figure 23), which emphasizes combustible gas detection and oxygen level monitoring, followed by pH testing. Greater familiarity with physical mitigation techniques than with chemical mitigation techniques is apparent both in the lesser availability of ionization and vapor detectors in Figure 23, and in the severe drop in the number of responders with neutralizers or solidifiers as opposed to containment and confinement items in Figure 24.

Flaws in the Data

While the AAI survey provides a new perspective on response capabilities, some flaws in the data are likely to exist. Foremost among these may be the various interpretations possible in Section 4 on Training (see Figure 13), where the instructions read "List the total number of personnel currently trained to the levels listed below. Do not include anyone who has not received initial and/or refresher training in the past two years." Because the survey did not specify to count each person only once (for the non-ICS training), the number of Technicians may also have been counted in Operations, and Operations in Awareness. Consequently, Awareness or Operations level personnel may be over-represented.

The main problem, though, is that identifying the components that potentially make a team qualified to respond at a given level does not make a team. Teams are formed through agreements, plans, contracts and exercises. Most of the response organizations contacted have such agreements, and depending on who those agreements are with and the conditions imposed, may or may not be qualified, willing or able to respond.

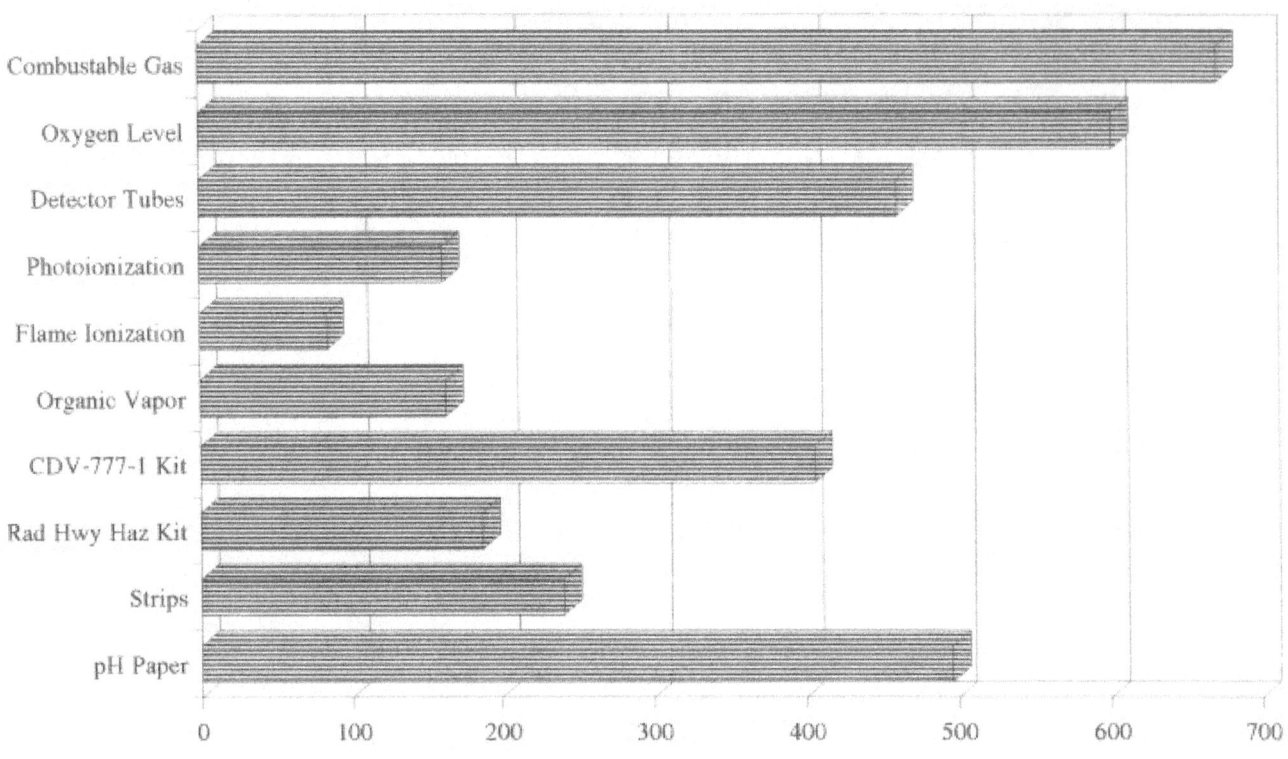

Figure 23. Team detector capabilities. Source: Abkowitz and Associates, Inc, 1994.

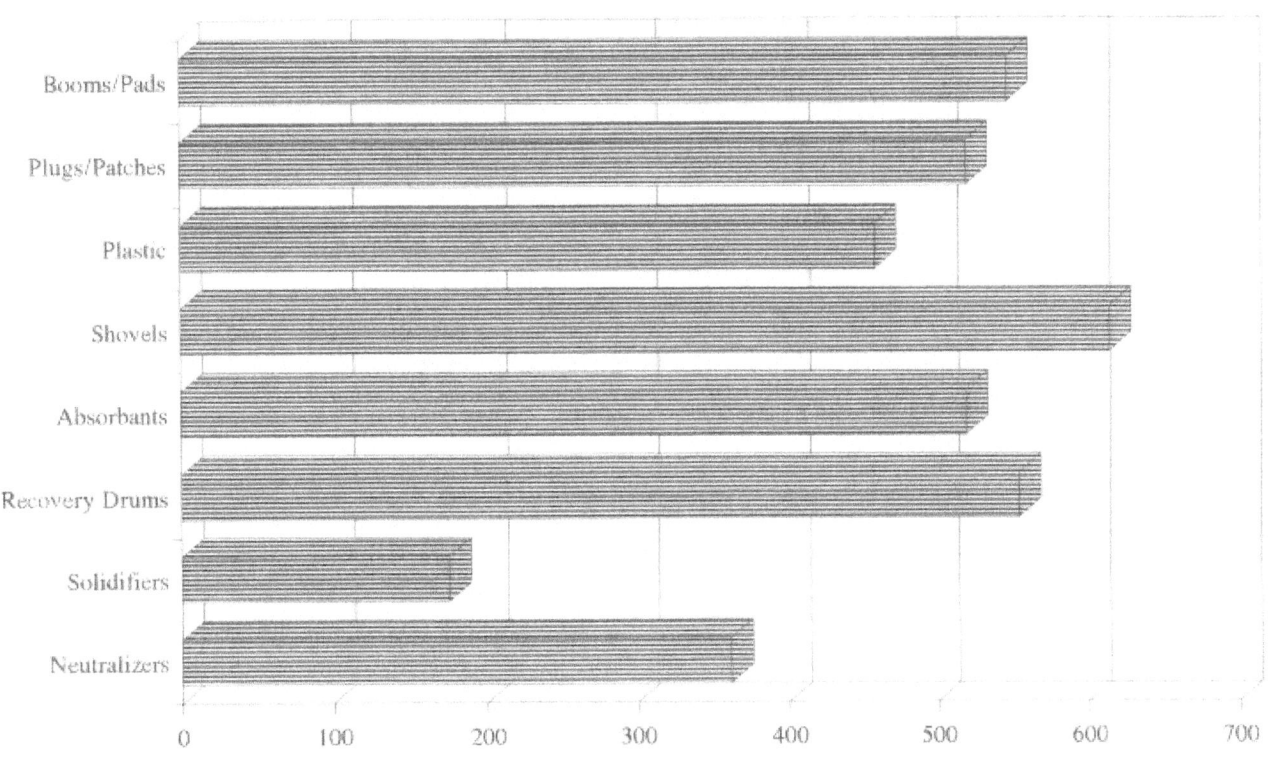

Figure 24. Team containment capabilities. Source: Abkowitz and Associates, Inc, 1994

CHAPTER III

NATURE OF THE PROBLEM: HAZARDOUS MATERIALS RELEASES

Data Sources

There have been 270,000 Emergency Response Notification System (ERNS) reports from late 1986 to April 1994.[22] ERNS is especially relevant for national emergency response preparedness because it records all notifications at the time they are telephoned in to the National Response Center. Data from the 130 ERNS fields is relayed to the appropriate EPA Regional office, and is the basis for determining the level of response dispatched. 17 percent of ERNS notifications are CERCLA hazardous substances, with 41 percent for petroleum-based oils and 12 percent for non-petroleum-based oils (see Figure 25).[23] Significantly, at the time of reporting an incident, the nature of 30 percent of released substances is "other" or "unknown."

ERNS data does not present the full picture, however. Non-CERCLA hazardous substances are not required to be reported to the National Response Center, and SARA Title III reporting requirements for facilities direct them to report to State Emergency Response Commissions and Local Emergency Planning Committees only (see Figure 2).

Number of Releases

Of the 270,000 releases reported in ERNS by April 1994, more than 160,000 had been recorded for the Federal fiscal years (FY) 1987-1991, the latest for which national statistics were available.[24] Over that five year period, petroleum and its derivatives registered 64,974 reports; hazardous substances, 27,977; and non-petroleum oils 18,611

---

[22]Michael B. Cusick, ABB Environmental Services, Inc. (contractor with EPA ERNS information requests), telephone interview April 12, 1994.

[23]EPA, Oil Notifications: Emergency Response Notification System (ERNS) Fact Sheet (Publication 9360.0-22FS), April 1992

[24]All ERNS statistics cited in this thesis were obtained through Freedom of Information Act requests by the author.

270,000 Notifications by Material Type to April 1994

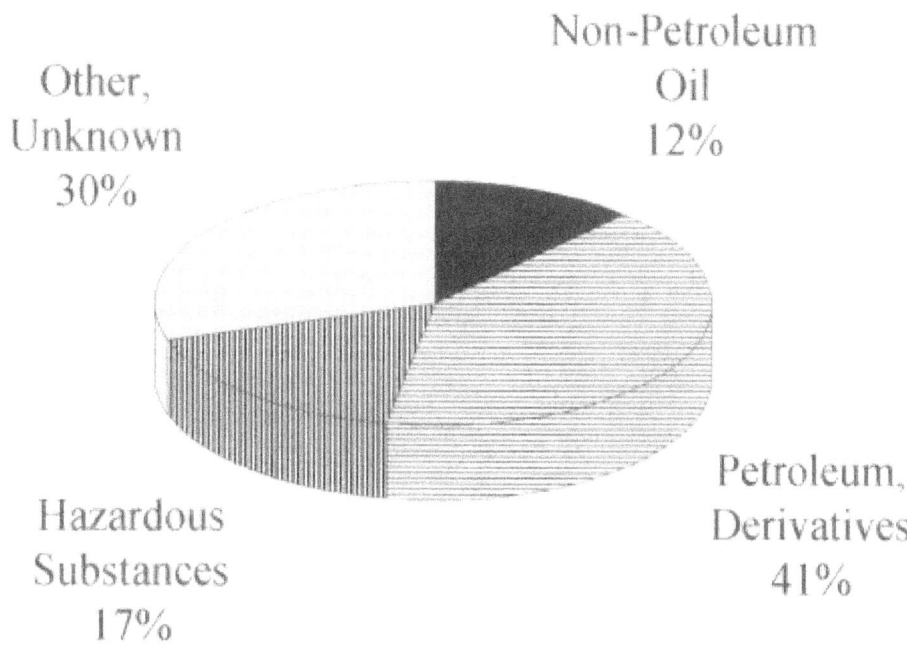

Figure 25. 270,000 ERNS notifications by material type, to April 1994. Source: EPA, 1994

(see Figure 26). The types and quantities of reported releases are fairly constant from year to year, as seen in Figure 27, indicating a continuing, consistent need for capable response.

Magnitude of Releases

Releases of less than 1,000 gallons dominate petroleum spills, with releases in excess of 100,000 gallons representing an average of 0.2 percent of notifications (see Figure 28).[25] A similar pattern holds for non-petroleum oils (not shown). While CERCLA notifications are similarly dominated by releases of less than 1,000 *pounds*, releases of more than 100,000 pounds constitute more than 1 percent of notifications, as seen in Figure 29. Since the seriousness of a release (and, therefore, the level of response) is partially determined by release magnitude, the dominance of small releases implies that lesser-qualified teams may be able to successfully mitigate the majority of releases.

Distributions of Releases

Geographic

Reported releases for FY87-FY91 are not distributed evenly across the 10 EPA Regions. Region 6 (Arkansas, Louisiana, New Mexico, Oklahoma and Texas) dominates, accounting for roughly 20 percent of CERCLA notifications and 30 percent of petroleum and non-petroleum oil notifications, as seen in Figure 30. Region 6 has 30,000-plus notifications, followed by Region 9 (Arizona, California, Nevada, Hawaii) with less than 20,000. Regions 3, 4 and 5 are in the 10,000 to 15,000 range, with the remaining regions under 7,500 notifications. A map of the 10 EPA Regions is provided as Figure 31.

Federal reporting requirements have remained relatively steady for the last three years (FY91, FY92 and FY93). Region 6 detailed data is explored for these years.

---

[25]EPA, Oil Notifications: Emergency Response Notification System (ERNS) Fact Sheet (Publication 9360.0-22FS), April 1992.

Notifications (1987-1991) By Material Type

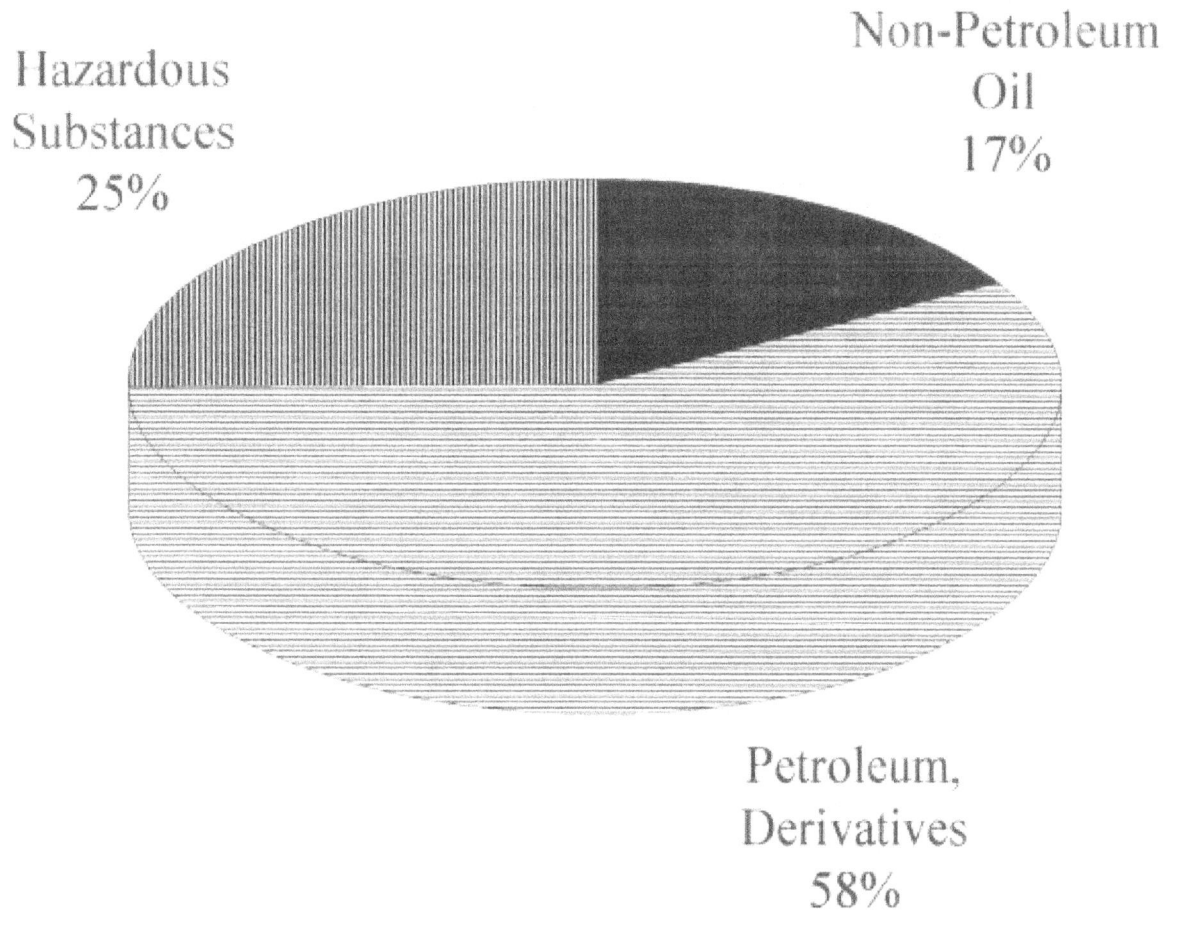

Non-Petroleum
Oil
17%

Hazardous
Substances
25%

Petroleum,
Derivatives
58%

Figure 26. ERNS notifications FY87-FY91 where material type is known. Source: EPA, 1994.

Notifications By Material Type

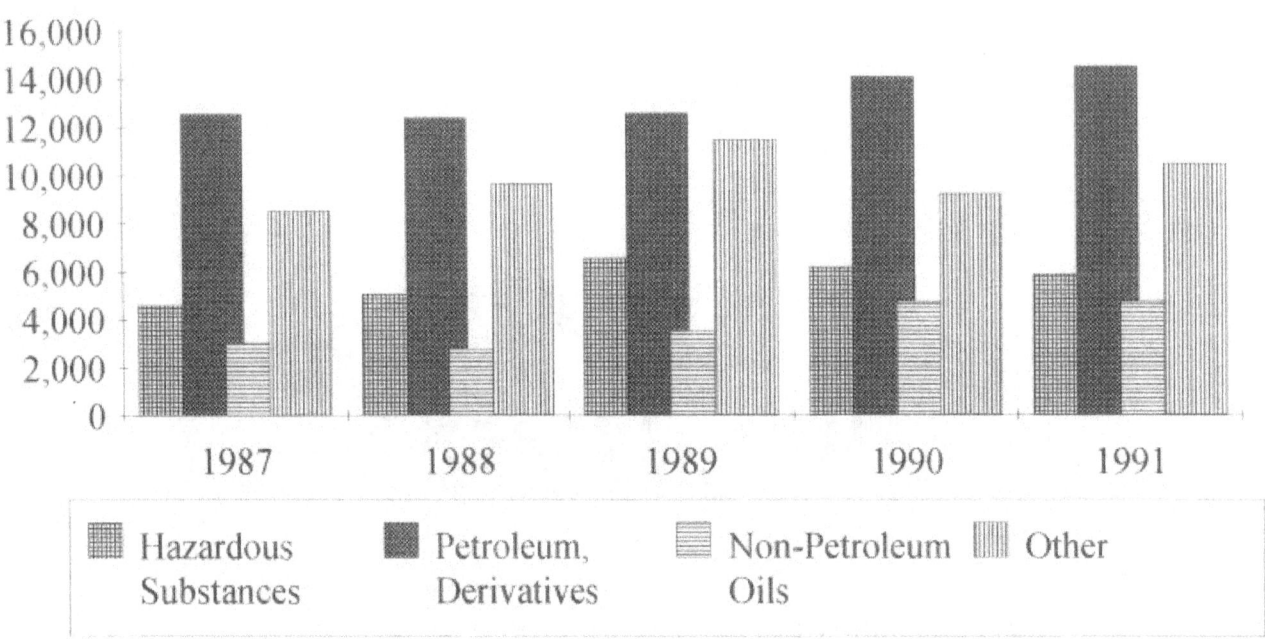

Figure 27. ERNS notifications by material type. Source. EPA, 1994

Number of Petroleum, Derivatives Notifications By Size

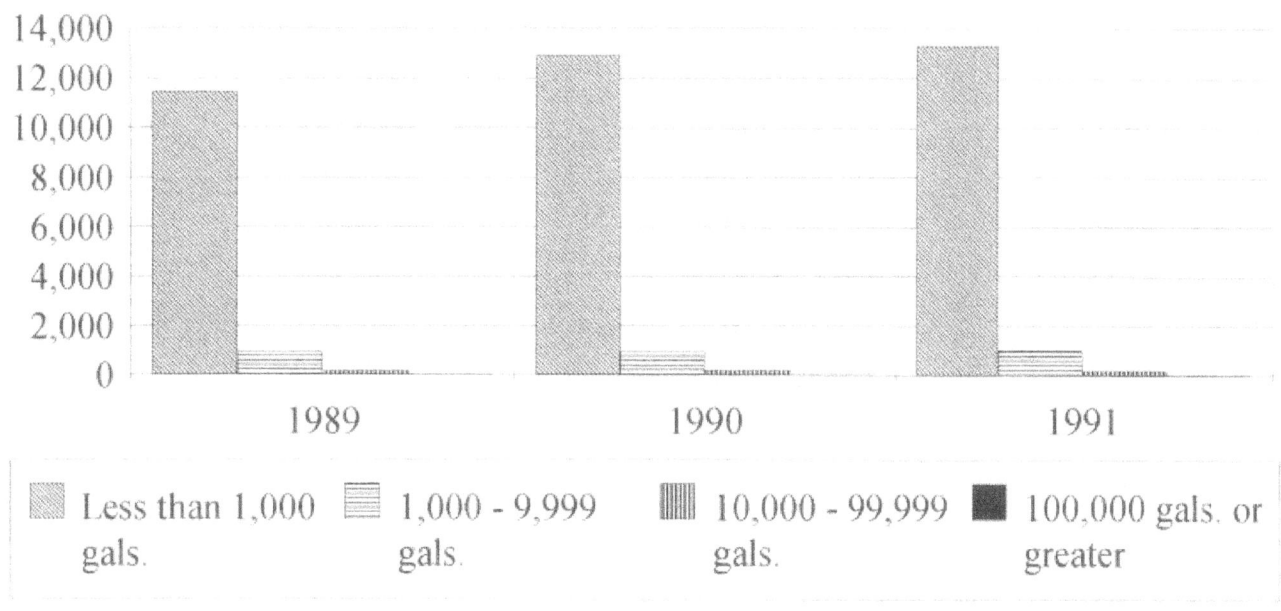

Figure 28. ERNS petroleum notifications by size. Source EPA, 1994.

Number of CERCLA Hazardous Substance Notifications
By Quantity

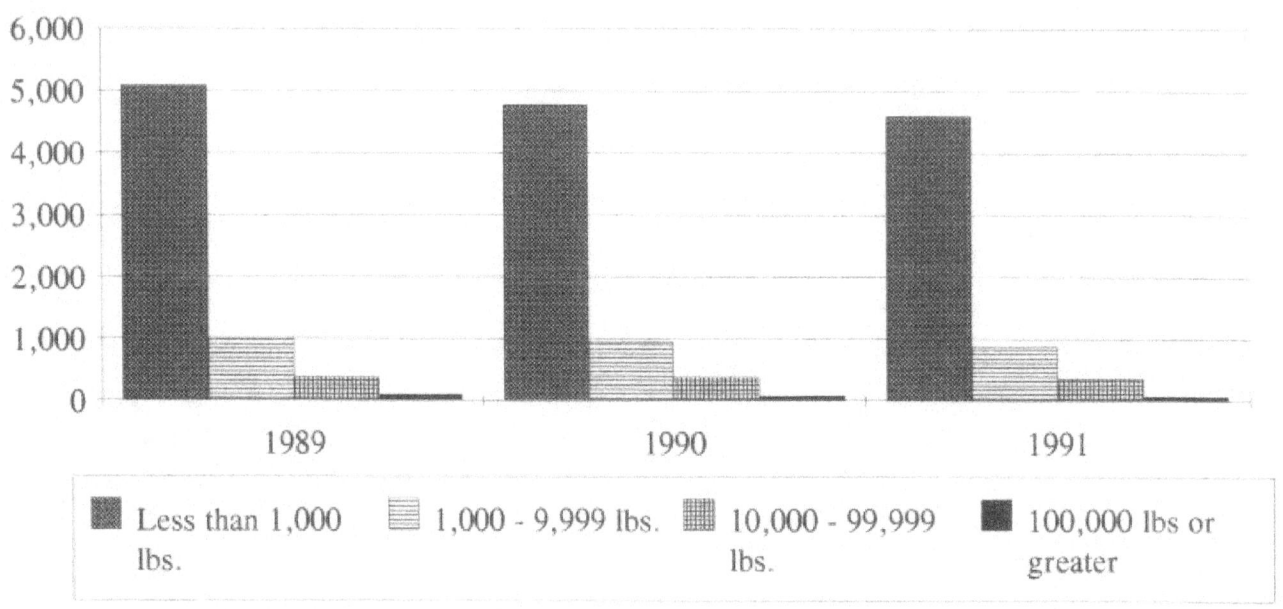

Figure 29. ERNS hazardous substance notifications by quantity. Source: EPA, 1994.

Notifications (1987-1991) by U.S. EPA Region

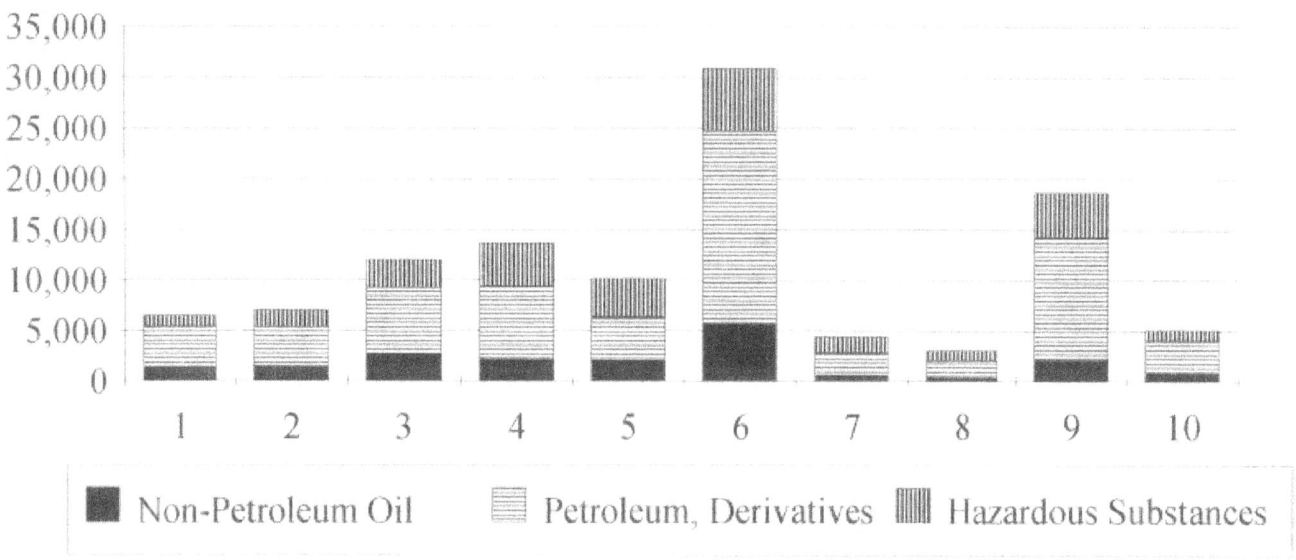

Figure 30. ERNS notifications FY87-FY91 by EPA Region. Source. EPA, 1994

Figure 31. EPA Region boundaries. Source: Chemical Manufacturers Association, *TRANSCAER® Guide*, n.d., p E-6a.

There is wide variation in the number of notifications by state within a region, as typified in Figure 32. The non-uniform nature of release distributions by locale is dramatized in the number of notifications by county or parish, as shown in Figure 33. Harris County, which dominates this list, is the home of Houston (two other Houston-area counties are also among the top 15). These figures suggest that response needs will vary significantly from jurisdiction to jurisdiction.

By Substance

Again looking at FY93 reported releases for Region 6, crude oil has a dominating lead with 923 notifications (see Figure 34), followed by a handful of hazardous substances clustered in the 150 to 170 notifications range (see Figure 35). Hazardous substance releases dwindle by type much less precipitously than do oil releases, indicating a need for chemical-specific training and equipment for relatively infrequent events.

By Source

Nearly three out of four reported releases in Region 6 for FY93 were at fixed facilities (see Figure 36), which under EPCRA are required to provide emergency notifications and to have emergency response plans (see Figure 2). Only seven percent occurred on highways, and four percent on rail transportation.

By Cause

About 70 percent of Region 6 reported releases are caused by equipment failure (see Figure 37). Nearly half these equipment failures are caused by valves, flanges or hoses, as shown in Figure 38. These causes suggest the need for Specialist level responders, familiar with the specific equipment involved, in responding to fixed facility releases.

Transportation related releases are dominated by (highway) collisions and overturns, as seen in Figure 39. "While multiple-vehicle collisions represent 47 percent of the accidents for trucks carrying hazardous materials, these accidents result in only 16 percent of all hazmat releases. Single-vehicle collisions represent 53 percent of the

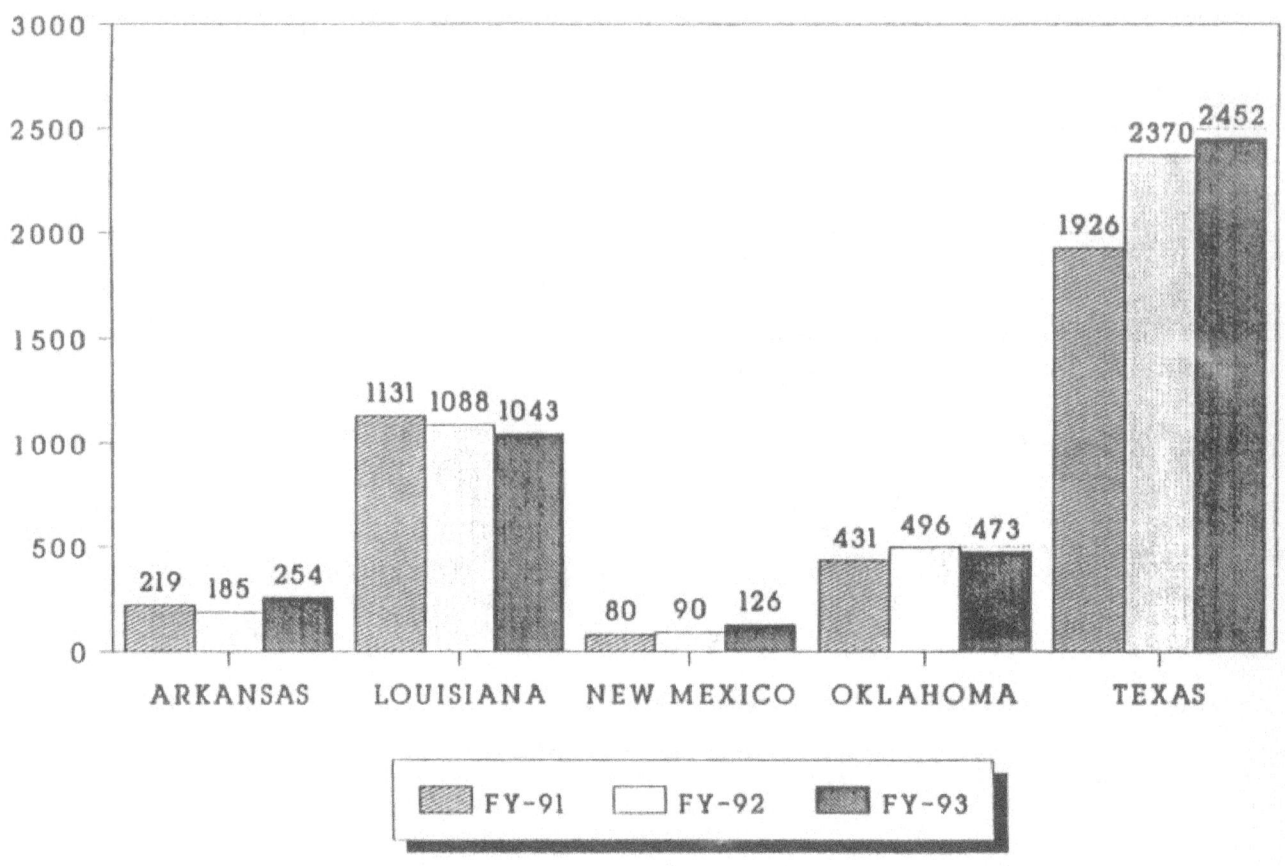

Figure 32. ERNS notifications by state. Source: EPA Region 6, 1994.

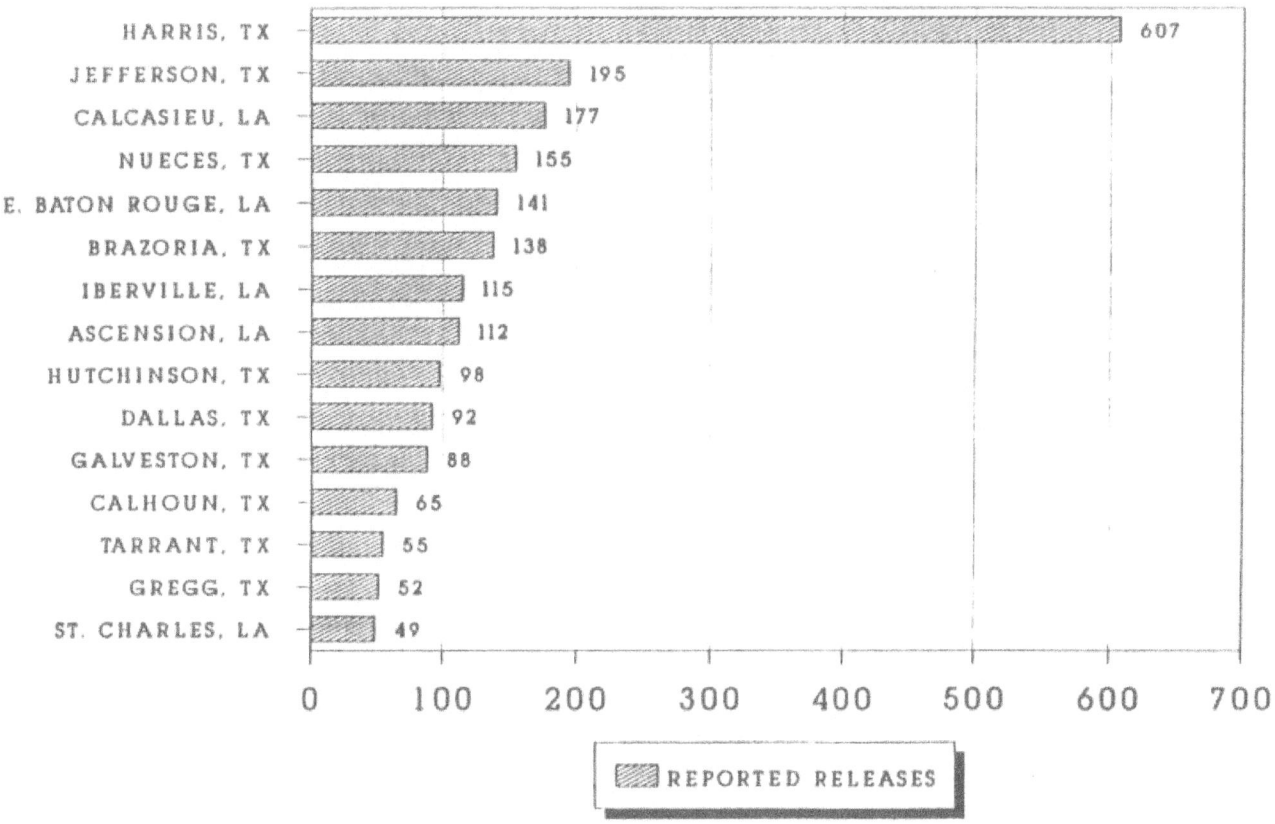

Figure 33. ERNS Top 15 counties/parishes reported releases - Region 6. Source: EPA Region 6, 1994

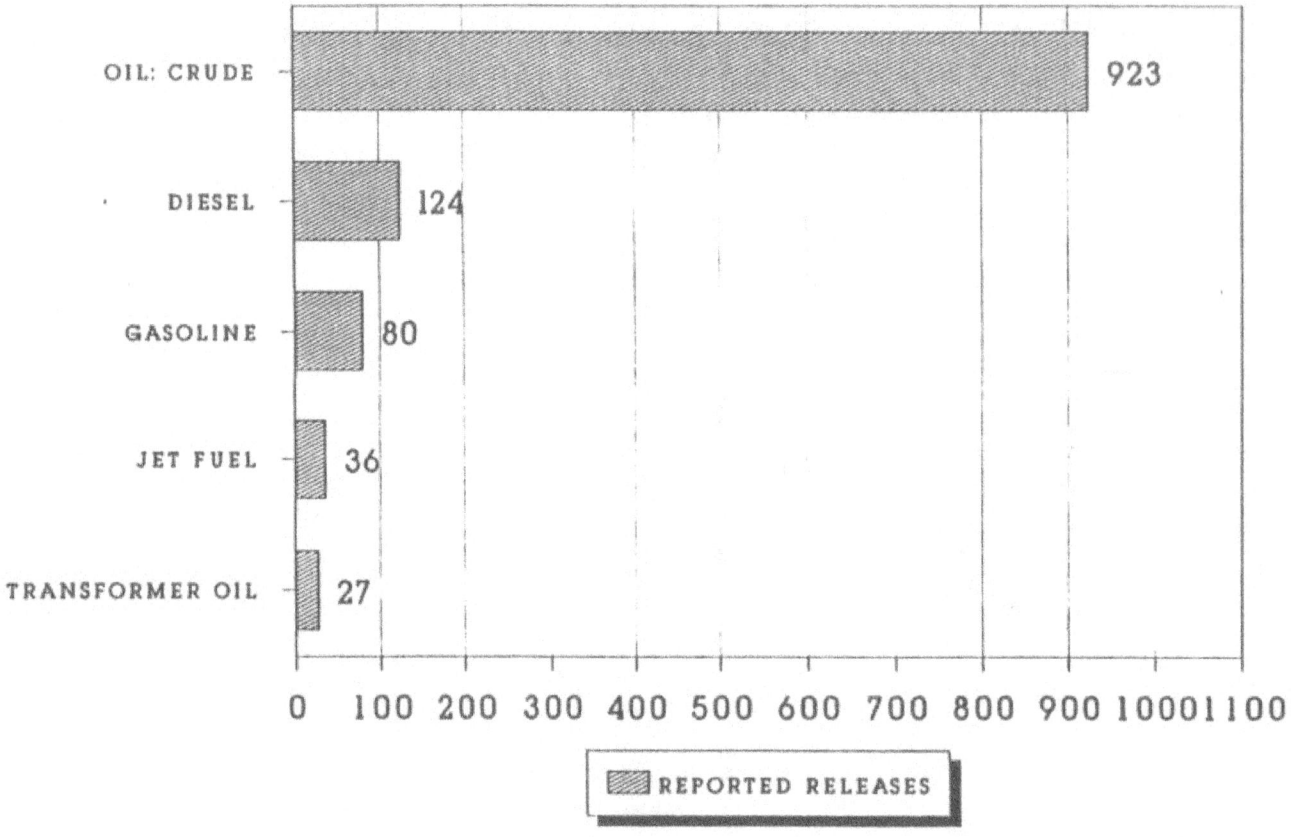

Figure 34. ERNS Top 5 oil products reported releases - Region 6. Source: EPA Region 6, 1994.

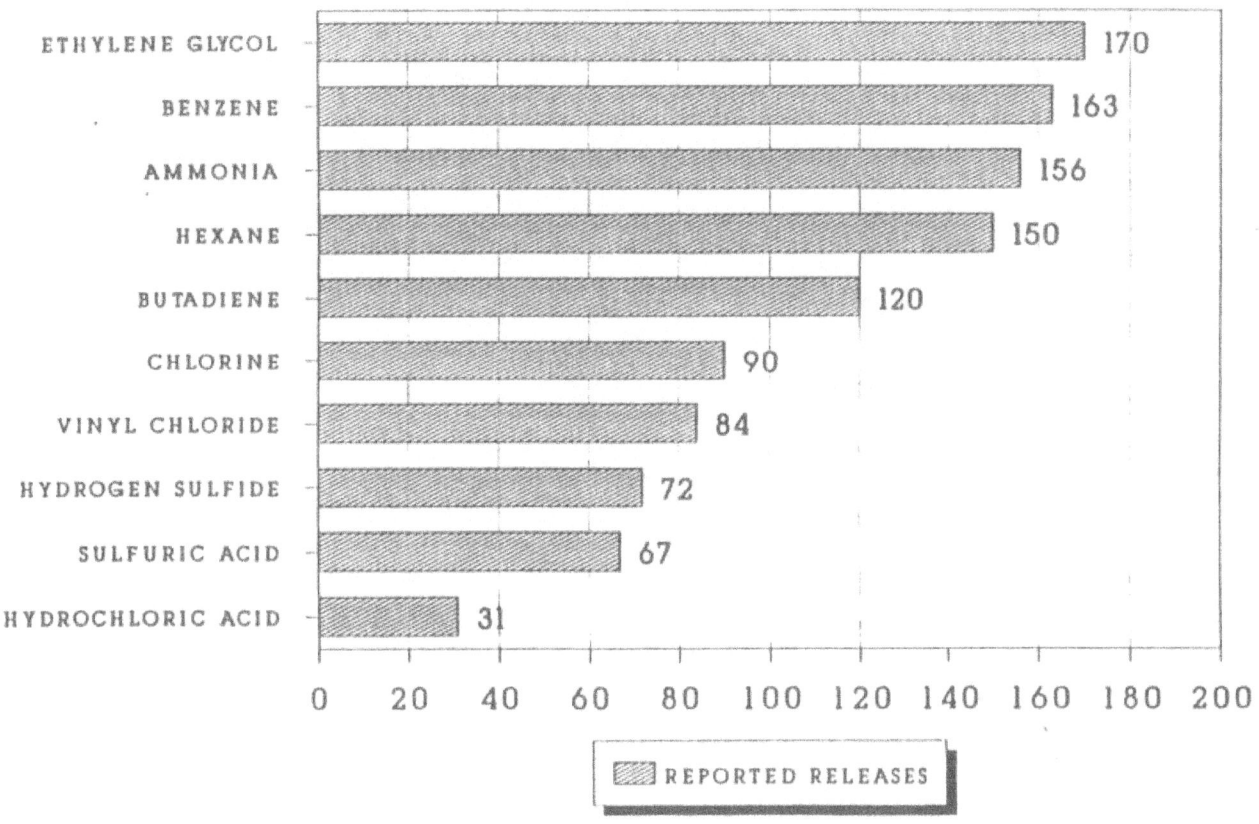

Figure 35. ERNS Top 10 hazardous substances reported releases - Region 6. Source: EPA Region 6, 1994.

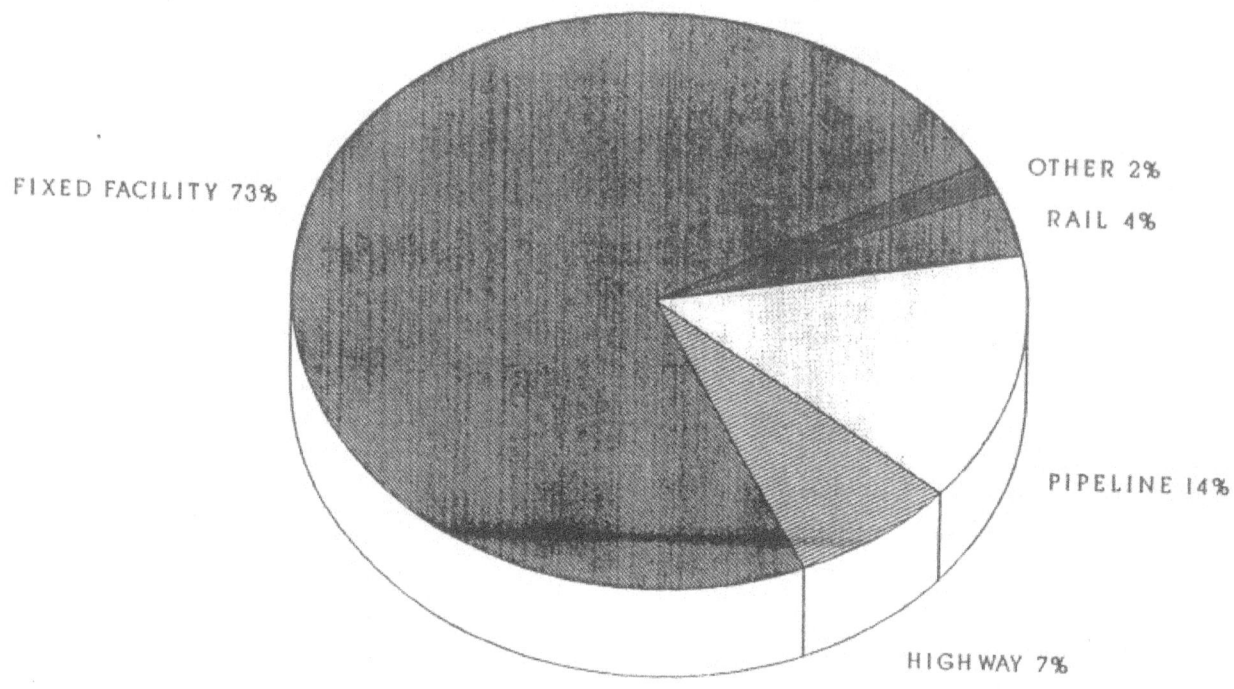

OTHER • UST, OFFSHORE, AIR, VESSEL

Figure 36. ERNS Sources of reported releases - Region 6. Source: EPA Region 6, 1994.

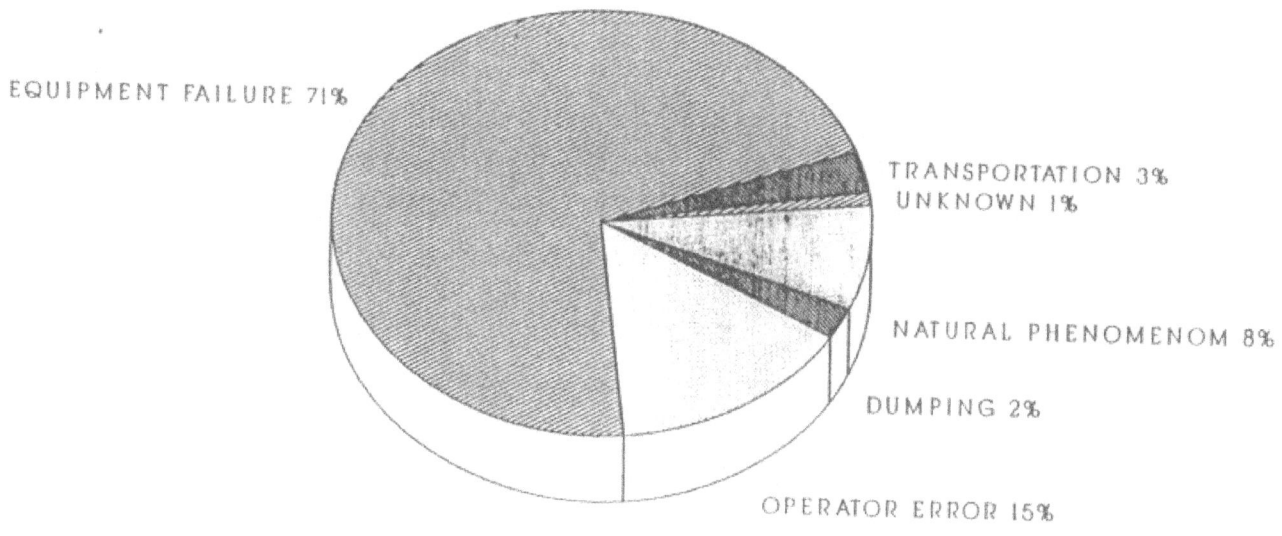

Figure 37. ERNS Cause of reported releases - Region 6. Source: EPA Region 6, 1994

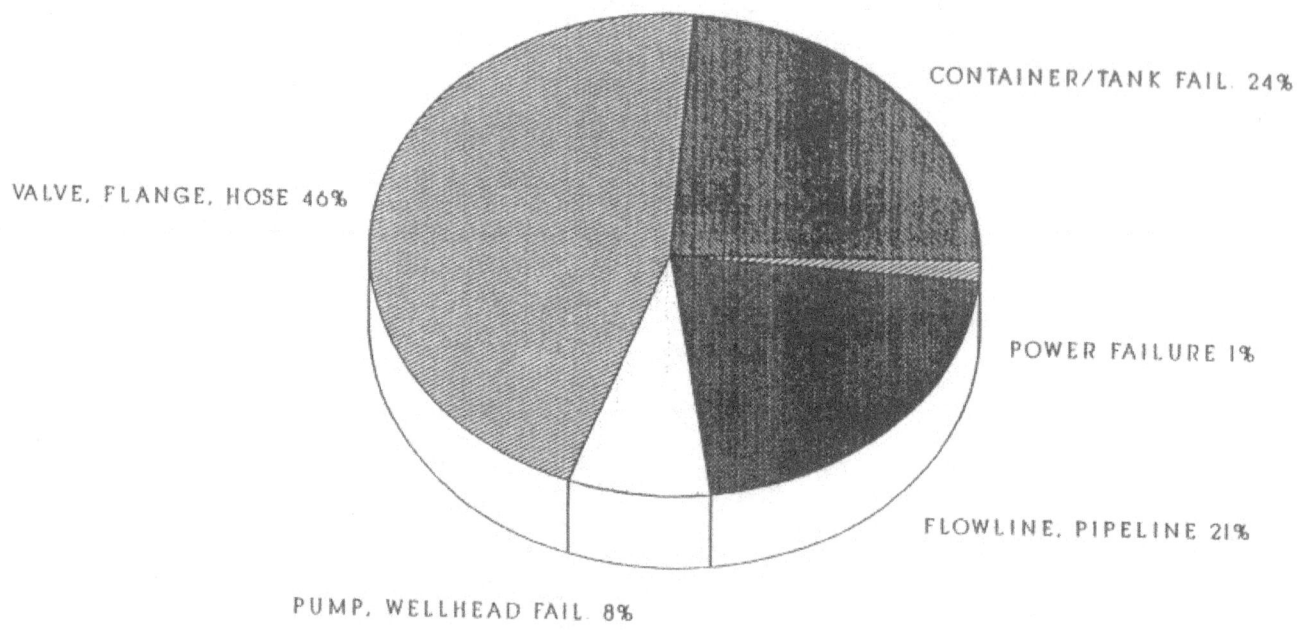

Figure 38. ERNS Cause - equipment related reported releases - Region 6. Source: EPA Region 6, 1994.

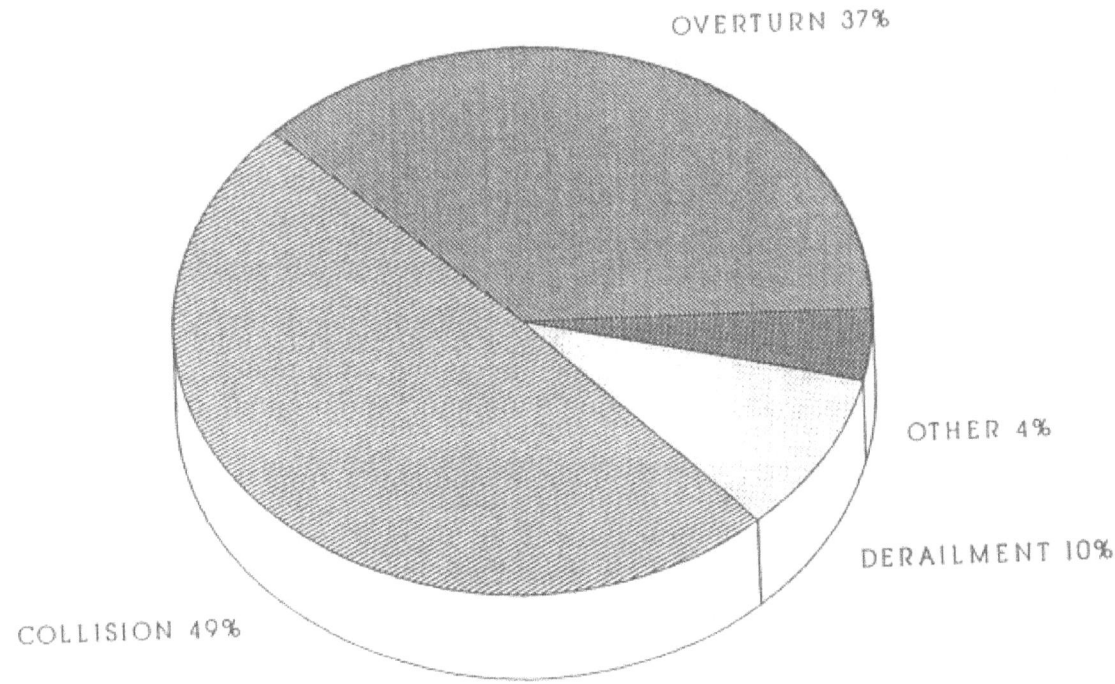

Figure 39. ERNS Cause - transportation related reported releases - Region 6. Source: EPA Region 6, 1994.

accidents for trucks carrying hazardous materials, but result in 84 percent of all [transportation] releases."[26]

Consequences

Region 6 represents roughly 28 percent of the ERNS notifications FY87-FY91. Multiplying the results of Region 6 notifications by 3.6 should therefore roughly approximate the number of evacuations, deaths and injuries nationally (using the reasonable assumption that consequences are proportionate to the number of releases). The FY91 results for Region 6 (see Figure 40), multiplied by 3.6, yield 252 evacuations, 216 deaths, and 1,034 injuries nationally.

While FY91 values are the highest of the four most recent years, the number of evacuations and injuries are typical. The 60 (unconfirmed) deaths reported in FY91 for Region 6 are atypical (14, 21, 15 the other years), but not particularly suspect given the number of reports, the magnitude of injuries, and the unconfirmed nature of the ERNS-reported deaths.

It is important to remember that these consequences of nationally reported releases are reported at the time of notification; they reflect outcomes contemporaneous with the releasing event. They do not include chronic effects, or effects on responders subsequent to ERNS notification.

---

[26]Harwood et al.. "Characteristics of Accidents and Incidents in Highway Transportation of Hazardous Materials," *Transportation of Hazardous Materials 1989* (USA: National Research Council, Transportation Research Board, Transportation Research Record 1245), pp.27-28.

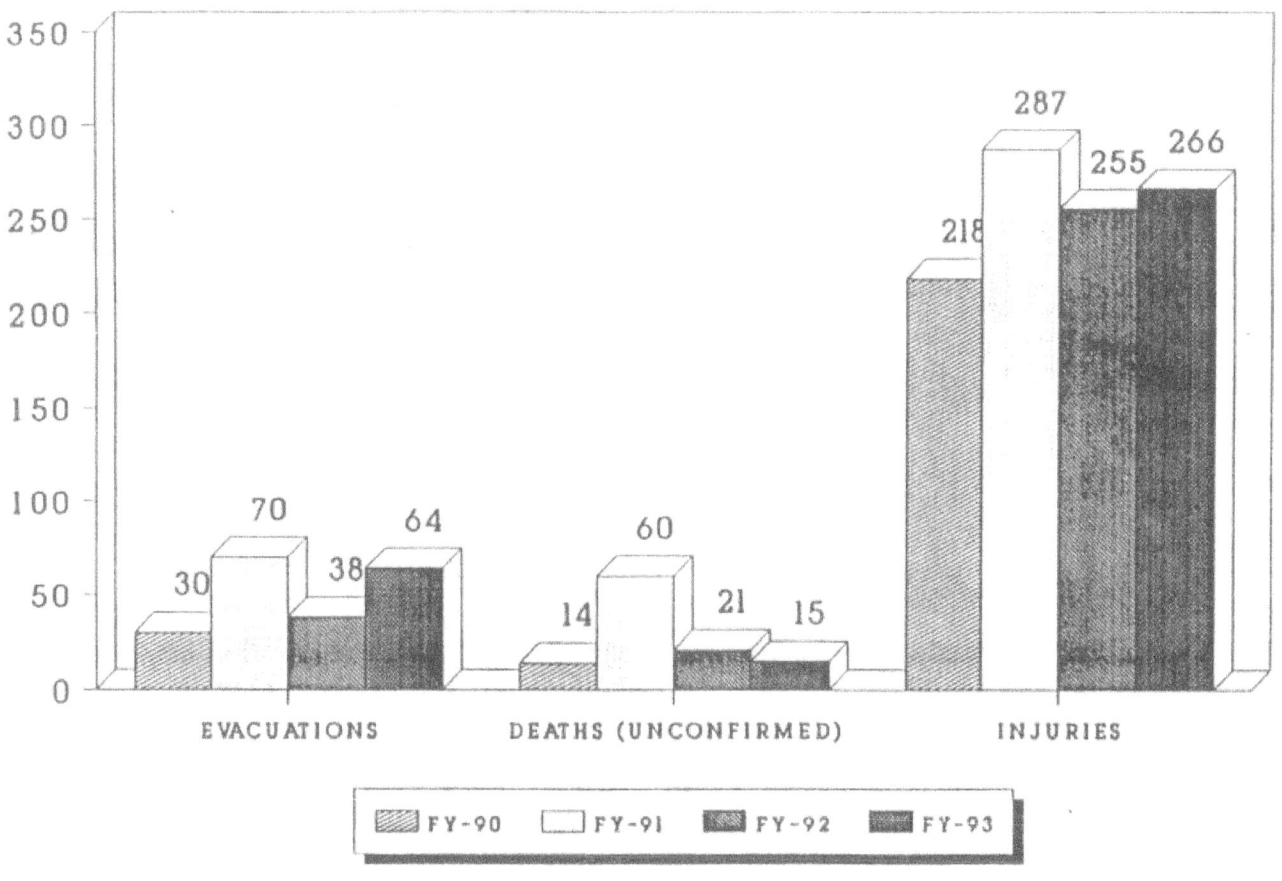

Figure 40. ERNS Results of notifications - Region 6. Source: EPA Region 6, 1994.

CHAPTER IV

SUMMARY AND CONCLUSIONS

Key Institutional Observations

Multi-Jurisdictional Tiered Response Is the Norm

Hazard-specific equipment and training requirements preclude all teams from being capable to handle all incidents. 600 out of the 700 surveyed responders with hazardous materials emergency mitigation responsibilities have multi-jurisdictional response agreements. Such agreements are common for fire fighting. Since most public hazardous materials response teams are based in fire departments, extending such agreements to hazardous materials response has been a small but critical step.

Up to 50 Agencies May Respond

An incident with large potential impacts may require coordinating the activities of dozens of responding agencies, including medical services, mass media, Red Cross, local public works departments, and wildlife management agencies (local, state and Federal). Relatively few of these agencies will have any contact with the hazardous materials, but all appropriate arrangements need to be anticipated in local emergency response plans. The process itself is at least as important as the plan, because planning together fosters communication and establishes response roles, including boundaries.

Survey Findings

Appropriate Response Preparedness

Appropriate response is specific to the situation. Local emergency planning is a tool to define appropriate response for anticipated hazards. The Federal approach requires each local jurisdiction to decide what level of local public capability is appropriate. Federal legislation requiring such preparedness was propelled by the local government maxim "perception is reality." Thus, the local governmental entities that fund public responders may prepare for locally-perceived risks from hazardous materials, in accordance with other pressing public needs in the local community. The uneven distribution of reported releases strongly suggests great variability in the local needs for public response capability. At a bare minimum, all members of the first responder community (fire fighters, law enforcement officers, emergency medical technicians) should have Awareness level training.

The public/private nature of overlapping response capabilities suggested in the planning process is supported in the data, as the most capable public response teams include Specialist level personnel. Since three out of four releases take place at fixed facilities, those privately owned fixed facilities will likely supplement local public response with facility-specific experts from the private sector, who bring with them perspectives only gained through experience.

Assessment of Preparedness

Roughly 600 public response teams are identified through the 1994 AAI survey data, which is a significant increase from the 130 public teams identified in 1985. National notification levels of releases have remained fairly steady over the substantial portion of this period for which data is available, suggesting that response capability is likely to have increased relative to the calls for response.

Response capabilities are atomized, and it is suggested by the National Fire Protection Association (NFPA) that they remain so. The NFPA explicitly refrains from defining team competencies, instead applying competency level designations to individuals.[27] Furthermore, the NFPA rejects the equation of training plus equipment equals competence.[28] Competence includes judgment, and team competence needs to be made by the incident commander. Perfect information is never available, and it is the responsibility of the incident commander to weigh all relevant facts and evidence for a

---

[27]NFPA, *Hazardous Materials Response Handbook*, Gary Tokle, ed., 1993, p.109.
[28]NFPA, *Hazardous Materials Response Handbook*, Gary Tokle, ed., 1993, p.114.

specific situation, taking into account not only the training and equipment, but also demonstrated competence through recent, relevant experience.

As with response team competence, assessing preparedness requires judgment. As such, it combines the assessor's past experience, personal opinion, and analysis of the data.

Response Time Improvements

In theory, the tiered response approach makes each of the 30,000 fire departments part of a national hazardous materials emergency response team. Those fire departments with the Awareness capabilities to identify, isolate and notify are the first responders on the national "team." The significant reduction in average notification time for Region 6 from 9 hours in FY90 to less than 4 hours in FY93 (see Figure 41) implies that the national "team" has improved its response time by 5 hours. Although this change is significant, there remains room for more improvement.

Policy Implications

Federal Policies Are Effective

In 1985, hazardous materials emergency response preparedness was perceived as inadequate. Public emotional discontent was likely fueled by the lack of consolidated information as much as by the scope and nature of the risks posed. Federal initiatives since 1985 have emphasized consolidated statistical reporting, and appear to have effectively: (1) addressed the accident and release prevention segments of hazardous materials risk management, and (2) reduced the consequences of hazardous materials releases through improved hazardous materials emergency response (implied by the significant reduction in notification times and increased response team competencies).

Together, these Federal approaches address the causes as well as the effects of hazardous materials releases. This has allowed policy makers to make informed decisions

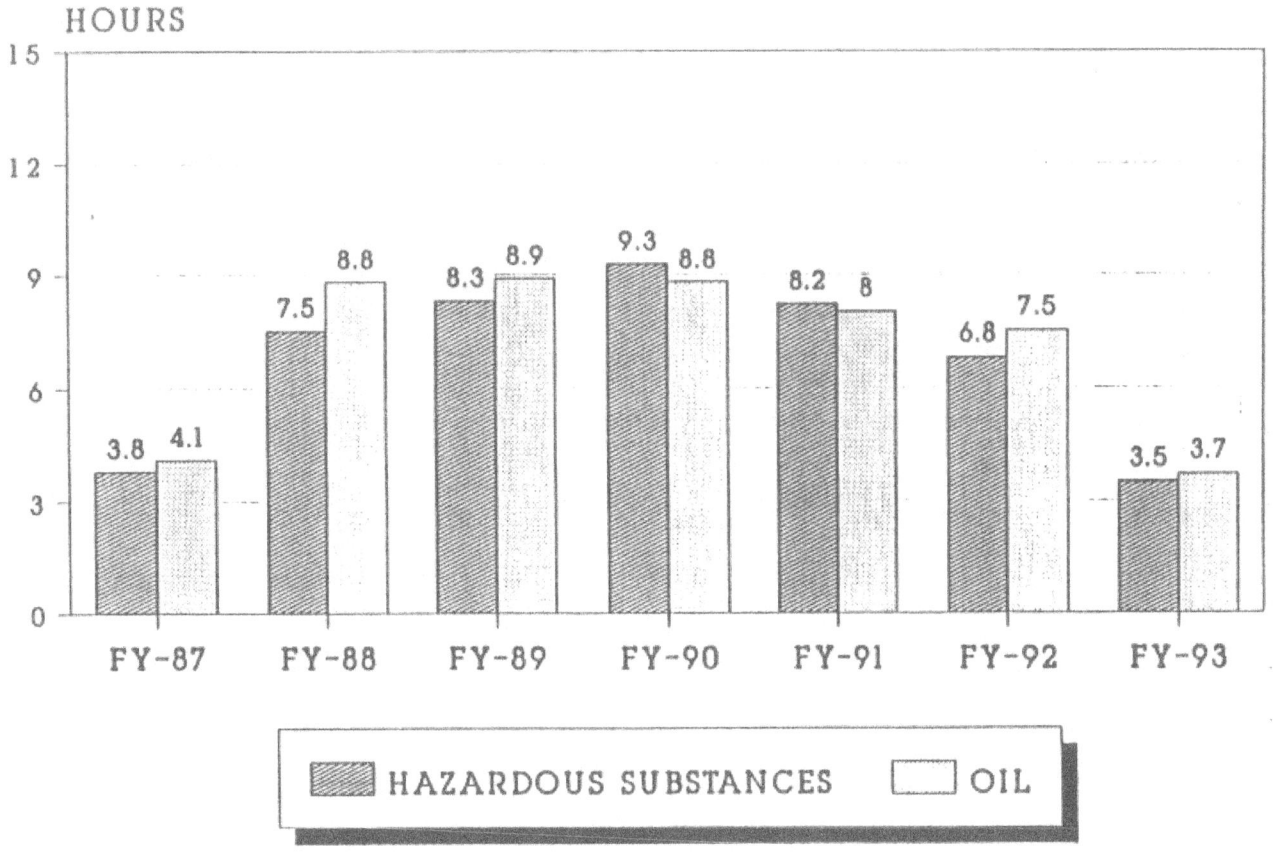

Figure 41. ERNS Average notification time in hours - Region 6. Source: EPA Region 6, 1994.

as to what are reasonable risks, and how much response preparedness is justified in their local jurisdiction.

Planning and Training Efforts Need to be Sustained

To this end, there is a Federal interest in seeing that local emergency response plans are exercised and evaluated. Consolidated exercise requirements presently under development[29] will need to be enforced to be effective. Such plans are likely to be taken seriously only where there are fixed facilities subject to EPCRA requirements, however.

Training of all emergency responders to the Awareness level is essential. To effectively address the fears and uncertainties that accompany hazardous materials in jurisdictions without fixed facilities upon which to focus Local Emergency Planning Committee attention, Awareness level training is doubly important.

Directions for Future Research

A study of local emergency management plans, perhaps through a survey asking for the local evaluation of the plans as exercised, would potentially provide insight into the adequacy of preparedness in jurisdictions with fixed facilities. Local perceptions drove the demand for legislation, which led to emergency planning requirements; local perception should, therefore, be the measure of the adequacy of local preparedness. Training of all first responders to Awareness level needs to be a monitored goal. A statistically valid survey verifying fire fighter training to at least the Awareness level at the 30,000 fire departments would be a good start. Planning and training studies might be conducted nationally, regionally, or on a state-by-state basis, and could potentially be conducted concurrently.

---

[29]The National Preparedness for Response Exercise Program (PREP) is a unified Federal effort and incorporates the exercise requirements of the Coast Guard, the Environmental Protection Agency, the Research and Special Programs Administration Office of Pipeline Safety and the Minerals Management Service. As of October 1993 the PREP addressed the exercise requirements for oil pollution only; regulations for hazardous substance releases were under development, and those requirements will be incorporated into the PREP once completed. Source: National Preparedness for Response Exercise Program (PREP) Guidelines. Draft 10/1/93 (presumably a Coast Guard document).

APPENDIX A

VERIFICATION FORM

Hazardous Materials Emergency Response Survey Verification

Location ——————————————————————

County:

City:

Region:

Classification ——————————————————————

Public   Private   Industry

General Information ——————————————————————

Dept./Company:

Mailing Address:

City: State: Zip:

Street Address (where equipment is kept):

Team Leader: Business Phone:

No. Paid: No. Volunteer:

No. Assigned to Team: No. Responding to a Call: Emergency:

Avg. Response Time: minutes

Geographic Location ——————————————————————

Longitude: Fax:

Latitude:

Jurisdictional/Company Profile ——————————————— 2. Jurisdiction

Total Population Served: Standard Area Served (square miles):

Major Highways (SR = State Route, I = Interstate):

Navigable Waters:

Major Railroads (by name):

Airports:

Written Multi-jurisdictional Response Agreements   Written Industrial Mutual Aid Agreements

◯ Yes with: ◯ Yes with:

◯ No   ◯ No

Comments

Planning ——————————————————————— 3. Capabilities

Does the jurisdiction /company have an Emergency Management Plan? ◯ Yes ◯ No

Has the plan been successfully exercised and evaluated? ◯ Yes ◯ No

Date of last exercise: Date of next exercise, if avail.: 1/Jan/1994

Medical Surveillance ——————————————————————

Are team members presently participating in a medical surveillance
program in accordance with OSHA 1910.120? ◯ Yes ◯ No

Do you expect team members to participate in a medical surveillance
program in accordance with OSHA 1910.120 in 1994? ◯ Yes ◯ No

1228

Hazardous Materials Emergency Response Survey Page 2.

Training ———————————————————————————— 4. Training

List the total number of HazMat Response personnel currently trained to the NFPA levels listed below.
Do not include anyone who has not received initial and/or refresher training in the past two years.

Is the Senior Officer the Team Leader?   ◯ Yes   ◯ No

	Awareness	Operations	Technician	Specialist	Advanced (jurisdiction specific)	ICS
minimum hours of training:						
Senior Officer						
Team Leader(s)						
Team Members						
Support Personnel						
Totals						

Equipment ———————————————————————————— 5.1 Equipment

Please list the approximate number of pieces in the appropriate box.

PPE		Detectors		Respirators		Containment	
Turnouts (SFPC)		CombustableGas		30 minute SCBA units		Booms	
Level C		Oxygen Level		60 minute SCBA units		Pads	
Level B		Detector Tube Kits		Air Line		Plugs/Wedges	
Level A		Photoionization		1/2 Mask Cartridge		Patches	
Fire Res Coveralls		Flame Ionization		Full Mask Cartridge		Plastic Rolls	
Proximity Suit		Organic Vapor		45 minute SCBA units		Shovels	
Disposable Suits		CDV-777-1 Kit		Extra SCBA Cylinders:		Absorbants (lbs.)	
Cooling Vests		Rad Hwy Haz Kit		30 minute		Recovery Drums	
Nuclear Suits		Strips		60 minute		Solidifier Kits	
		pH Test		45 minute		Neutralizer (gallons)	
						Spill Kits	
						FloatingWaterPump	

Available Transportation ————————————————————   5.2 Equipment

No. Equipped Trucks: _____   No. Heavy Equipment: _____   Non-Sparking Tools? ◯ Yes ◯ No

No. Aircraft: _____   No. Special Vehicles: _____   Decontamination? ◯ Yes ◯ No

SCBA Refill (no. by type) ————————————   Foam (no. of gallons) ——————————

Cascade: [ ] Fixed [ ] Portable   Alcohol: [ ]   Protein: [ ]

Compressor: [ ] Fixed [ ] Portable   Light Water: [ ]   Other: [ ]

Type: [ ]

Reference Books ————————————————————

No. Ref. Books in vehicle: [ ]   List of additional references:

DOT P 5800.5   ◯ Yes
1990 ERG or later: ◯ No

1228

65

Stephan Alexander Parker

Hazardous Materials Emergency Response Survey Verification Page 3.

Communications ————————————————————————— Comm/InfMgt

Cellular Phones ——————————— Radio Bands ———————————————
Phone numbers: Band(s)/Frequency(s):
No.:   No.:

Facsimile Machines —————————————————————————————
Stationary ———————————   Portable ———————————
No.:   Fax numbers: No.:   Fax numbers:

Information Management —————————————————————————————
                Computers   Stationary   Portable
        IBM compatible:
           Apple/Mac:

Programs ——————————————————————————————————————
        ☐ Cameo   ☐ Archie   ☐ Plume Modeling   ☐ EIS

        Names of other programs:

Survey Originally Completed by: ———————————————————— Completed By
            Name:
       Title/Rank:
    Phone Number:

This Verification Completed by: ———————————————————— Verified By
            Name: _____
       Title/Rank: _____
    Phone Number: _____   Date: _____

66

APPENDIX B

CHEMTREC BROCHURE

Materials Transportation Act Amendments of 1984. CHEMTREC also enjoys a close working relationship with the National Response Center (NRC) and notifies the NRC of significant incidents. In turn, the NRC notifies CHEMTREC of major releases of hazardous materials, and in some cases, requests CHEMTREC's assistance in responding to these situations.

NONEMERGENCY SERVICES

CHEMTREC expanded its public services in 1985 and added toll-free nonemergency telephone lines to provide the general public, chemical users, industrial workers and others with access to nonemergency health, safety and environmental information about chemicals and chemical products. The Center's toll-free number for nonemergency information is 1-800-262-8200 and can be reached from anywhere in the United States and Canada. The line is staffed Monday through Friday from 9 a.m. to 6 p.m. Eastern time.

LENDING LIBRARY & TRAINING ACTIVITIES

CHEMTREC also addresses the needs of the emergency response community through its Emergency Response Training initiatives. In 1985, CHEMTREC established a Lending Library of audio-visual training programs for personnel responding to hazardous materials emergencies. Library materials are available at no cost to anyone in the United States who wishes to borrow them.

The programs, several of which have been developed by a group of emergency response experts from CMA member companies, provide responders with specific technical information and advice to assist them in safely mitigating incidents involving a wide variety of hazardous materials.

CHEMTREC also regularly conducts "hands-on" workshops for emergency responders and makes its services available for emergency response drills and simulations. The goal is to ensure that when problems do occur, emergency responders know what to do and how to promptly obtain expert technical assistance from the chemical industry.

RESPONSIBLE CARE®

CHEMTREC is an important component of CMA's Responsible Care® initiative, through which member companies have made a commitment to continually improve the industry's performance in health, safety and environmental quality. This includes increased emphasis on the safe transportation of chemicals, emergency preparedness and accident prevention, and providing emergency advice and assistance in the event an incident involving chemicals occurs.

USER GUIDANCE

CHEMTREC can provide pertinent information and guidance in situations when given only the NAME OF THE PRODUCT or the NATURE OF THE PROBLEM. For more detailed information and assistance, or if the product is initially unknown, attempt to provide as much of the following information as possible:

- Name of Caller and Call Back Number
- Location of Incident
- Shipper or Manufacturer's Name
- Container Type
- Railcar or Truck Number
- Carrier Name
- Consignee
- Local Conditions

Limit calls to CHEMTREC's emergency telephone number, 1-800-424-9300, to emergency situations only. Please do not tie up the emergency telephone lines unnecessarily.

For nonemergency questions, general information, or to obtain information on any of CHEMTREC's services, call 1-800-262-8200.

Written inquiries should be sent to:

CHEMTREC
c/o CMA
2501 M Street, NW
Washington, DC 20037

FOR CHEMICAL EMERGENCY
Spill, Leak, Fire, Exposure or Accident
CALL CHEMTREC DAY OR NIGHT
800-424-9300

Toll Free in the United States, Canada, Puerto Rico and the Virgin Islands

For Emergency Calls Originating Outside the United States:
202-483-7616
(Collect Calls are Accepted)
All Calls are Recorded

For Nonemergency Information:
800-262-8200

CMA
CHEMICAL
MANUFACTURERS
ASSOCIATION

68

BACKGROUND

CHEMTREC® is a public service established by the Chemical Manufacturers Association (CMA) and its members in 1971 to provide first responders, the transportation industry, medical professionals, and others with access to response information and technical assistance from chemical industry experts for incidents involving hazardous materials.

The Center was developed as both a resource for obtaining immediate emergency response information to mitigate accidental chemical releases, and as a means for emergency responders to obtain technical assistance from chemical industry product safety specialists, emergency response coordinators, toxicologists, physicians and other industry experts to safely mitigate incidents involving chemicals.

The CHEMTREC Center can be reached from anywhere in the United States, Canada, Puerto Rico and the Virgin Islands, through its toll-free emergency telephone number, 1-800-424-9300. Callers outside the United States and ships at sea can contact the Center using CHEMTREC's international and maritime number, 1-202-483-7616 (collect calls are accepted).

The CHEMTREC emergency telephone number is displayed on a variety of containers carrying hazardous materials, including rail cars and tank trucks, so that in a chemical emergency, first responders and others at the scene can immediately contact CHEMTREC for assistance. The CHEMTREC emergency telephone number is also displayed on hazardous materials shipping papers by companies that are registered with CHEMTREC as a method of compliance with U.S. Department of Transportation Hazardous Materials Regulations.

While the majority of the Center's activity involves providing assistance for hazardous materials transportation emergencies, it also provides support in handling nontransportation and medical incidents.

MODE OF OPERATION

CHEMTREC's emergency center is staffed 24 hours a day, seven days a week by trained communicators. CHEMTREC can contact the majority of major chemical manufacturers and thousands of chemical shippers and distributors. The Center can also contact hundreds of carriers who may be transporting these materials for additional information and assistance. CHEMTREC has the capability to teleconference the onscene incident commander or emergency responder with representatives of the shipper or manufacturer, medical professionals, poison control center specialists and other technical experts to obtain immediate advice and assistance. The Center can conference 25 telephone lines simultaneously, if necessary.

The Center uses a two step approach in handling emergencies involving hazardous materials:

First, on receipt of a call, the communicator on duty records information relative to the incident such as the caller's name, organization, telephone number, location of the incident, shipper and consignee, carrier, product name, nature of the incident, (i.e., spill, leak, fire or exposure). Based on this and any additional information the caller is able to supply, the CHEMTREC communicator provides immediate emergency response information for the chemical(s) involved. This information is generally provided from a manufacturer's product specific Material Safety Data Sheet (MSDS).

Second, details of the incident are relayed to the 24-hour emergency contact designated by the shipper or manufacturer. The shipper is expected to contact the incident scene to provide any additional follow-up technical advice and assistance, including dispatching personnel to the scene if required.

Where limited information is available, CHEMTREC can still assist using other resources, such as its network of carrier and company contacts and its extensive reference library.

Identification of the shipper and product name in an emergency is an important step in minimizing the time required to provide necessary information and assistance. Shipping papers that accompany shipments of hazardous materials for all modes of transportation are the primary source of this information. If they are unavailable, railcar and truck numbers and carrier names can be extremely useful in identifying cargoes and shippers.

CHEMTREC maintains a reference library of over 1,000,000 MSDSs. The information on a product can be accessed from the communicator's workstation within seconds and faxed immediately to response personnel at the scene of a hazardous materials incident. In this manner, emergency responders operating at the emergency scene have access to CHEMTREC's entire MSDS library.

MUTUAL AID PROGRAMS

CHEMTREC serves as the communications link for several industry product specific mutual aid programs. These mutual aid programs are formal arrangements between chemical companies to respond to incidents on one another's behalf. Agreements exist for specific products including Chlorine, Phosphorus, Hydrogen Fluoride, Hydrogen Cyanide, Hydrogen Peroxide, and Vinyl Chloride. Similar arrangements cover shipments of compressed gases, swimming pool chemicals and liquefied petroleum gas.

In 1985, CHEMTREC expanded its emergency response mission and established the Chemical Industry Mutual Aid Network to address those commodities not covered by one of the product specific mutual aid plans. The network is comprised of emergency response teams from participating chemical companies and teams provided by commercial, for-hire contractors under contract to CMA. The primary objective of the program is to provide a chemical industry presence on the scene of chemical emergencies as soon as possible.

Membership provides a chemical company with around-the-clock access to a nationwide network of trained emergency response teams available to respond to an incident involving its product(s). If a shipper, who is a member of the mutual aid network, is notified by CHEMTREC that an incident involving one of its products has occurred and it is unable to respond promptly due to distance or other circumstances, CHEMTREC links the shipper with a response team closest to the scene able to provide assistance. This team responds to the incident on behalf of the shipper and renders assistance until the shipper can make arrangements to relieve the team. Responding teams are reimbursed for any expenses incurred by the shipper that requested their assistance.

RECOGNITION

Although CHEMTREC is a private industry sponsored program, its function and capabilities are formally recognized by the U.S. Department of Transportation (DOT) and a close working relationship exists between the Center and DOT. In fact, a formal memorandum of understanding signed by CMA and DOT in 1980 officially recognizes CHEMTREC as the central emergency response service for incidents involving the transportation of hazardous materials. This acknowledgement is included in the Hazardous

BIBLIOGRAPHY

Abensohn et al. "Environmental Crimes." *American Criminal Law Review* vol. 30:565, Spring 1993.

Chemical Manufacturers Association, CHEMTREC (brochure), n.d.

Comprehensive Environmental Response, Compensation, and Liability Act of 1980. Public Law 96-510. 42 United States Code 9601. December 11, 1980.

DOT/RSPA/OHMT-89-02. Guidelines for Applying Criteria to Designate Routes for Transporting Hazardous Materials, July 1989.

EPA. CERCLA Notifications: Emergency Response Notification System (ERNS) Fact Sheet (Publication 9360.0-23FS), April 1992.

EPA. Oil Notifications: Emergency Response Notification System (ERNS) Fact Sheet (Publication 9360.0-22FS), April 1992.

Federal Emergency Management Agency. *Digest of Federal Training in Hazardous Materials* (FEMA 134), June 1991.

Harrington, Lisa H. "The Last 30 Years," *Private Carrier*, January 1994, pp. 20-25.

Harwood et al. "Characteristics of Accidents and Incidents in Highway Transportation of Hazardous Materials," *Transportation of Hazardous Materials 1989*, USA: National Research Council, Transportation Research Board, Transportation Research Record 1245.

International Association of Fire Fighters. *A Nation at Risk: Emergency Response and the Transportation of Hazardous Materials.* Washington, DC: International Association of Fire Fighters, n.d.

Library of Congress. Congressional Research Service. Paul F. Rothberg. "Hazardous Materials Transportation Emergency Response Training and Planning Trust Fund: Concepts and Options." Washington, DC: November 10, 1988.

National Fire Protection Association. *Hazardous Materials Response Handbook.* Gary Tokle, ed. Quincy, Massachusetts: NFPA, 1993.

National Fire Protection Association. *Recommended Practice for Responding to Hazardous Materials Incidents*, NFPA No. 471. Quincy, Massachusetts: NFPA, 1992.

National Research Council. Committee for the Assessment of a National Hazardous Materials Shipments Identification System. *Hazardous Materials Shipment Information for Emergency Response.* USA: Transportation Research Board Special Report 239, National Academy of Sciences, 1993.

National Research Council. Committee on Risk Assessment Methodology. *Issues in Risk Assessment.* Washington, DC: National Academy Press, 1993.

National Research Council. Committee on Risk Perception and Communication. *Improving Risk Communication.* Washington, DC: National Academy Press, 1989.

National Response Team. *Criteria for Review of Hazardous Materials Emergency Plans* (NRT-1A). May, 1988.

National Response Team. *Hazardous Materials Emergency Planning Guide* (NRT-1). March, 1987.

NFPA. *Hazardous Materials Response Handbook.* Gary Tokle, ed. Quincy, Massachusetts: NFPA, 1993.

Subcommittee on Surface Transportation, Hazardous Materials Transportation, Senate Hearing 101-955, July 25, 1990.

Superfund Amendments and Reauthorization Act of 1986. Public Law 99-499. 42 United States Code 9601, Titles I-IV. October 17, 1986.

Title 49 of the Code of Federal Regulations, Chapter 1, Subchapter C: Hazardous Materials Regulations, Section 171.8; October 1, 1987.

TRANSCAER® Task Group, Chemical Manufacturers Association. (Seymour, T.H., P.E.) "Hazardous Waste Operations and Emergency Response: A Close-Up Look at Training." *TRANSCAER® Guidance Manual: An Industry Commitment to Public Safety.* Washington, D.C.: TRANSCAER® Task Group, Chemical Manufacturers Association, n.d. Reproduced from *Job Safety and Health Quarterly.* OSHA Training Requirements for Emergency Response Staff p. E-17.per 29 CFR 1910.120(q)(6).

U.S. Congress. Office of Technology Assessment. *Transportation of Hazardous Materials*. OTA-SET-304. Washington, DC: U.S. Government Printing Office, July 1986.

U.S. Congress. Senate. Committee on Commerce, Science and Transportation. Subcommittee on Surface Transportation. *Hazardous Materials Transportation*. Hearing, 100th Cong., 1st Sess. Washington, DC: U.S. Government Printing Office, 1987.

U.S. Department of Labor. Occupational Safety and Health Administration. *Hazardous Waste Operations and Emergency Response-Final Rule*. 29 Code of Federal Regulations Part 1910.120. Federal Register Vol. 54, No. 42, Part III. Washington, DC: Office of the Federal Register, March 6., 1989.

U.S. Department of Transportation. Federal Highway Administration. Office of Highway Information Management. *Our Nation's Highways: Selected Facts and Figures*, Publication No. FHWA-PL-92-004.

U.S. Department of Transportation. Research and Special Programs Administration. *An Overview of the Federal Regulatory Scheme for Hazardous Materials Transportation*, DOT/RSPA/OHMT-89/05.

U.S. Department of Transportation. Research and Special Programs Administration. Office of Hazardous Materials Transportation. *1987 Emergency Response Guidebook*, DOT P 5800.4, Washington DC, 1987.

U.S. Department of Transportation. Research and Special Programs Administration. Office of Hazardous Materials Transportation. *1990 Emergency Response Guidebook*, DOT P 5800.5, Washington DC, 1990.

U.S. Department of Transportation. Research and Special Programs Administration. Volpe National Transportation Systems Center. *Transportation Safety Information Report: 1991 Annual Summary*, DOT-VNTSC-RSPA-92-10, Washington DC: U.S. Government Printing Office, August 1992.

U.S. General Accounting Office. *Freight Trucking: Promising Approach for Predicting Carriers' Safety Risks*, GAO/PEMD-91-13, April 1991.

U.S. General Accounting Office. *Hazardous Materials: 1990 Transportation Uniform Safety Act--Status of DOT Implementing Actions*, GAO/RCED-92-55BR, November 1991.

U.S. General Accounting Office. *Pollution from Pipelines: DOT Lacks Prevention Program and Information for Timely Response*, GAO RCED-91-60, January 1991.

U.S. General Accounting Office. *Transportation Safety: Information Strategy Needed for Hazardous Materials*, GAO IMTEC-91-50, September 1991.

U.S. Nuclear Regulatory Commission. Office for Analysis and Evaluation of Operational Data. J.Jolicoeur. *Emergency Response Data System (ERDS) Implementation*, NUREG-1394, Washington, DC: April 1990.

Interviews

Cusick, Michael B. ABB Environmental Services, Inc. (contractor with EPA ERNS information requests), telephone interview April 12, 1994.

Manning, Howard. Manager, CHEMTREC Call Center. Telephone interview March 21, 1994.

Weaver, Wally. Director of Emergency Management Division, U.S. Department of Energy. Telephone interview July 14, 1993.

ABOUT THE AUTHOR

In 1994 and 1995, Mr. Parker filled more than 300 requests for complimentary copies of this report as a thank you for the cooperation received in filling out the surveys. As demand for copies has continued well beyond the dawn of the World Wide Web in 1995, the original document has been published to make it widely available through commercial channels.

From 1995 to 2000, Mr. Parker developed Intelligent Transportation Systems courses and ran the NTI Fellows program for the Advanced Technologies and Innovative Practices section at the National Transit Institute at Rutgers, The State University of New Jersey. He earned a BS in Speech from Northwestern University and an MS in Interdisciplinary Studies: Civil Engineering and Management of Technology from Vanderbilt University. Mr. Parker is author of *An Assessment of U.S. Hazardous Materials Emergency Response Preparedness* (MS thesis, Vanderbilt University, 1994) and co-author of *Technical and Sociopolitical Issues in Radioactive Waste Disposal, 1986* (The Royal Swedish Academy of Sciences, 1987). He served as Scholar Associate for a *Review of the Department of Homeland Security's Approach to Risk Analysis* (National Academy of Sciences, 2010).

Mr. Parker began his transportation career as a bus driver. As the Administrator for the Joint Powers Transportation Board of the Town of Jackson and Teton County, he served as the general manager for the START Bus transit system in Jackson Hole, Wyoming, and was founding vice-president of WYTRANS, the Wyoming Public Transit Association.

In 2010, Mr. Parker began developing the business case for Better-Drivers—remote piloting of vehicles by qualified operators. Presentations: (1) 2013 National Rural Intelligent Transportation Systems Conference, St. Cloud, Minnesota; (2) 2013 American Public Transportation Association's TransITech Conference, Phoenix, Arizona; (3) 2012 Intelligent Transportation Systems World Congress, Vienna, Austria.

In 2016, Mr. Parker's opera received its world premiere at the Mead Theatre Lab at Flashpoint in Washington, DC. *A Roadkill Opera* tells the story of the hour before the lights go up on opening night for a comedy improv troupe in 1988 Jackson Hole, Wyoming: the Roadkill On A Stick Frozen Foods Theatre Company. During that hour, they find out their showroom at the Silver Dollar Bar is being torn down. This original story and English libretto by Parker is set to music by Ferdinando Paer, Beethoven's direct competitor. 59 minutes (in English). The 2013 studio recording & sheet music for *A Roadkill Opera*, as well as the 2016 libretto, are available through your favorite bookseller.

www.ingramcontent.com/pod-product-compliance
Lightning Source LLC
Chambersburg PA
CBHW080625190526
45169CB00009B/3287